Jean Rhys

Literature and Life Series
[Formerly Modern Literature
and World Dramatists]

Selected list of titles:

*Complete list of titles in the series available from publisher
on request.*

Jean Rhys

Arnold E. Davidson

Frederick Ungar Publishing Co.
New York

Acknowledgments

I would first like to thank my wife, Dr. Cathy N. Davidson, for her contributions to this project and particularly for her patience during what in retrospect seem to have been interminable discussions on the art of Jean Rhys. My typist, Mrs. Betty Uphaus, also deserves special credit. With this manuscript, as with others, she did her usual superlative job. I am grateful, too, to the editors of *Contemporary Literature* and *Studies in the Novel* for allowing me to incorporate into this volume slightly revised versions of essays that first appeared in these two journals. Finally, I thank my colleagues—especially Professors Ken Bidle and Linda Wagner—and my students for the information, insights, and perspectives that they have provided me over the years.

Library of Congress Cataloging in Publication Data

Davidson, Arnold E., 1936–
    Jean Rhys.

    (Literature and life series)
    Bibliography: p.
    Includes index.
    1. Rhys, Jean—Criticism and interpretation. I. Title.
II. Series.
PR6035.H96Z63   1985   823'.912   84-28022
ISBN 0-8044-2143-9

Printed and bound in Great Britain by
Biddles Ltd, Guildford and King's Lynn

Contents

Chronology

1932   Divorces Jean Lenglet and marries Leslie Tilden Smith; publishes her translation of Edward de Nève's *Barred* (Jean Lenglet's novel, written under a pen name, and based on the same events that were the basis for Rhys's *Quartet*).

1934   Publishes *Voyage in the Dark*.

1936   Revisits the West Indies.

1939   Publishes *Good Morning, Midnight*.

1945   Leslie Tilden Smith dies; she is helped at the time of her husband's death by one of his cousins, Max Hamer.

1947   Marries Max Hamer.

1952   Max Hamer loses his position and serves a six-month prison sentence for misappropriating company funds.

1953   Moves, with her husband, to Cornwall.

1956   Moves to Cheriton FitzPaine, a small village in Devonshire which will remain Rhys's home for the rest of her life.

1957   BBC produces a radio dramatization of *Good Morning, Midnight* and advertises for information on the author; Rhys, thought by many to be dead, answers the advertisement and lets it be known that she is working on a new novel.

1964   Max Hamer dies; Rhys suffers a heart attack while bringing the almost completed manuscript of her new novel to London.

1966   Publishes *Wide Sargasso Sea*.

1967   *Wide Sargasso Sea* wins the W. H. Smith Award, the Arts Council of Great Britain Award for Writers, and the Heinemann Award of the Royal Society of Literature.

1968   Publishes *Tigers Are Better-Looking*.

1975   Publishes *My Day*.

1976   Publishes *Sleep It Off, Lady*.

1978   Is awarded the Commander of the Order of the British Empire for her contributions to literature.

1979   Dies May 14; *Smile Please: An Unfinished Autobiography* is published posthumously.

From Dominica to Obscurity and Fame

Late in her life Jean Rhys decided that her last task as a writer would be to record some of the details of the disordered past out of which her earlier novels had been written. She was in her mid-eighties at the time; her health was broken; she had never learned to type, and her hands were so stiff and gnarled by arthritis that she could hardly hold a pen. But she had become friends with David Plante, an American novelist living in London, and when she confided to him that "I wanted to write about my life, I wanted to write my autobiography, because everything they say about me is wrong. I want to tell the truth," he agreed to serve as her amanuensis.[1] For three years he and a few others too assisted her on the volume that was still not fully completed to her satisfaction when she died in the spring of 1979. In that same year her last work, *Smile Please: An Unfinished Autobiography*, was published posthumously.

Unfinished as it is, the book can hardly succeed in its purpose "to put the record straight."[2] Diana Athill, who had been Rhys's friend and editor for over twenty years and who prepared *Smile Please* for publication after Rhys's death, also observes in her forward to the volume that the second half of the autobiography describing Rhys's life after she had left the West Indies at age sixteen to live in Europe is particularly fragmentary. So the author provides no clear, coherent account of the most

disordered time of her chaotic existence, and the temptation still remains to read her life according to the circumstances of her different protagonists and vice versa.
Indeed, Rhys's own retrospective account of crucial
events such as her first affair or her subsequent abortion
almost exactly parallel her fictional rendering of those
same events. Every autobiography is, of course, a partial
fictionalization of the remembered past. But the problem
is compounded for an autobiographer such as Rhys who
has already so thoroughly fictionalized so much of her
past.[3] Thus the writer in her forties creates the protagonist of *Voyage in the Dark*, Anna Morgan, out of
memories of her own first affair and abandonment, and
over forty years later she well may have created still
another version of her twenty-year-old self simply by
transposing that forty-year-old rendering back to biography.[4] In short, instead of clarifying distinctions between the author's life and her biographically based
stories and novels, *Smile Please* only further confuses the
fictional with the factual.

That confusion will not be resolved until a
thoroughly researched biography is published. And Rhys
definitely represents an intriguing challenge for some
industrious biographer. But even if a future definitive
"life" could answer all the critic's hard questions as to just
what determined this author's subject matter and shaped
her idiosyncratic style, it is still doubtful that such a biography would add much to the general reader's apprecia-
tion of the novels.[5] We already know the basic details of
the writer's past and, more specifically, how Rhys herself
viewed that past. Furthermore, and as I have suggested
elsewhere, the "real life of an imaginative writer" is that
life as the writer "imagines it to be."[6] Rhys writes out of
her own experience, yet that experience is not simply
what happens to her but what happened as she perceives
it. The "is" of fact is from the first inextricably conjoined
with the fiction of "seems."

What I am arguing is that *Smile Please*, for all its limitations, is an appropriate introduction to this author's biography. The main events of the life, presented in disconnected fashion, duplicate the manner in which they were experienced. It is as if Rhys, always concerned with the shape of her work, had worked out a form appropriate for a nearly formless life. Furthermore and in another sense, even the lacunae at the heart of her own account of her various setbacks have a calculated effectiveness, for those very gaps and blanks return us to the novels, and it is only the novels that finally, as Rhys herself insisted, matter.[7] But before considering the novels themselves I shall briefly assess the general outline of the life as set forth in *Smile Please*. I also begin with *Smile Please* because the "fragmentary" and "impressionistic" (in Athill's terms) nature of this memoir make it an appropriate introduction to Rhys's impressionistic art.

The art of the autobiography is especially obvious in the portion that Rhys substantially completed, the first half telling of her early life in Dominica where she was born in 1890 and lived until she was sixteen. Consider, for example, how she begins her account with the childhood memory that gives the volume its title: "'SMILE PLEASE,' the man said. 'Not quite so serious.'" The six-year-old girl, dressed in her birthday finery, was having her photograph taken. At the wrong minute she moves. So the photograph–very much like the life–hardly turns out as intended. But the author's portrait of herself as a young girl, as much as the photographer's, symbolically foreshadows her life to come. Thus the frowning child prefigures the disappointments and disasters that the adult protagonist will subsequently suffer, while the photographer's admonition anticipates the cavalier style in which most of those same setbacks will be endured.

The opening episode is significant and significantly placed for still another reason. Rhys's first "clear connected memory" of her past life leads directly to her first clear realization of the transitory nature of that life. The memory is of her white dress and her new black shoes, of being especially happy while at the family's beautiful estate in the hills, of having the birthday picture taken. The realization comes three years later when she can no longer recognize herself in the photo: "I remembered the dress she was wearing, so much prettier than anything I had now, but the curls, the dimples surely belonged to somebody else. The eyes were a stranger's eyes . . . she wasn't me any longer. It was the first time I was aware of time, change and the longing for the past." What the nine-year-old girl first begins to perceive, the woman almost ninety telling that story knows all too well.

The story is mostly of the passing of time, the predominance of loss, the prevalence of longing. And the story begins, for the child, long before she recognizes that it is under way. By the time she is nine, for example, her family no longer owned the "beautiful, wild, lonely, remote" mountain-surrounded vacation retreat where she had been so happy when she was six. The family itself had already begun to break up. Her two older brothers were at school in England and her older sister was living with an aunt on another Caribbean island. Another child had been born into the family to claim most of the mother's attention. The larger world was becoming less accommodating too. A brooding, unfriendly nurse charged with the young girl's care perpetually dwelt on the dangers of both the natural and the supernatural world. Looking back some eighty years later, Rhys can conclude, "Meta had shown me a world of fear and distrust, and I am still in that world." Sent to a Catholic convent school where "white girls were very much in the minority," she encounters the obverse of prejudice, an "impersonal, implacable" animosity that proves, to the child, "we are hated."

The relationship between whites and blacks in Rhy's

life and fiction, as in William Faulkner's, is complicated and could itself be the subject of an extended study. Briefly put, she knew that her mother's grandfather had been a slave-owner, and consequently "the Lockharts, even in my day, were never very popular." She knew, too, that his estate had been burnt after the Emancipation Act by newly freed Negroes. On the other hand, her first close friend was black, and she was apparently mothered by some of the black servants (Meta excepted) as much as she was by her own mother. She remembered praying "ardently" as a small child "to be black" and recognizing later as a young girl how much her "growing wariness of black people" was tinged with "envy"; "I decided that they had a better time than we did. . . . They were stronger than we were. . . . They were more alive, more a part of the place than we were." On a seeming paradisical tropical island, a fall into the real world was well under way. One obvious aspect of that fall is the young girl's growing suspicion that social divisions and distinctions do not necessarily correspond to natural ones. This is a recognition that will help her when she is later placed, at least socially speaking, among the lower orders and it is also the basis for a quality first recognized by Ford Madox Ford in Rhys's first fiction but obvious in all of her work—her "passion for stating the case of the under-dog."[8]

There were three alternatives and escapes for the child who "dreaded growing up" in the narrow world of white West Indian society. She began to see her doctor father, in this setting, as a "sad man, continually brooding over his exile in a small Caribbean island," her mother as "a stranger in a strange house . . . lonely, patient and re-signed." The problem was to avoid that pattern. But the first imagined escape—"to be black and to dance . . . in the sun"—was obviously never going to materialize. The second was literature. One teacher at the Catholic school instilled in her a "love of words, especially beautiful words," and she began to read French and English poetry extensively, particularly the latter. English literature perhaps suggested the third escape, to leave the colonial imitation for England itself. This she decided to do at age sixteen. Her father's sister was visiting from London. Arrangements were made for the young girl to sail from Dominica with her aunt. Her father's parting advice was to warn her that "it's going to be very different" in England and she would "have to get used to that." She was to write him if she was "very unhappy, or want[ed] anything very much," but not "at the first shock."

That shock came on the gray day when the ship docked. At her first view of England–Southampton seen through a porthole–her "heart sank" and she "knew for one instant all that would happen to me." She liked London no better. The tourist sites to which she was taken did not evoke the proper response of admiration or awe. She found Westminster Abbey to be a "muddle"; St. Paul's to be "too cold, too Protestant"; the London Zoo gave her "such an impression of hopeless misery that I couldn't bear to look." These intimations proved prophetic. Rhys, as an adult, never could comfortably accommodate herself to England or the English. Clearly, reversing her father's journey had not brought the daughter back to her ancestral home.

It is tempting to see in Rhys's protracted homelessness another example of an author finding in exile the necessary stance from which the writing can be done. That pattern was particularly validated in the early twentieth century by James Joyce's abandoning himself the Ireland that continued to occupy his fiction and then by all the young novelists who came to Paris in the twenties to write of other places. Nevertheless, it hardly applies to Jean Rhys who, as much as Ernest Hemingway or Samuel Beckett, also launched her career in Paris. To begin with and as already noted, she was not exactly at home as a child in the West Indies, and when some twenty-five years after she left she went back for her only return visit she was even less at home: "But there was nothing, nothing. . . . No, it wasn't as I remembered it." In short, homelessness, for Rhys, was not a matter of choice but a permanent condition. Second and equally important, Rhys long dwelt in English exile (and in other exiles too) with no intention of becoming a writer. So the novels are perhaps an unexpected by-product of the author's home-less state but not at all its anticipated result.

Nevertheless, her different non-homes and the differences between them do enter powerfully into Rhys's fiction. Louis James, himself a West Indian novelist, rightly observes that division marks all of Rhys's protagonists and works. Even those fictions ostensibly about only Europe, James argues, are pervaded by a "sensibility" shaped in the West Indies. Thus "Rhys expresses the archetypal conflict between the warm, sensuous tropics and the cold northern world."[9] Yet that opposition is complicated, James continues, by being superimposed on another one—the difference between the adult and the child. The Caribbean evokes the innocence of childhood; Europe suggests "adult responsibility . . . with the cruel compromise demanded by growing up."[10] What James does not point out is that with this double dichotomy each place must serve as a measure of the other's lack—and thus, by extension, of its own. For Rhys, the adult dilemma is far more complicated than the question of which is preferable—to be warm and callow or wise and cold.

Rhys as a young adult was often both callow and cold. She had come to England to complete her education but soon decided that she would be an actress. She wrote her father for permission, and, true to his earlier word, he gave it, whereupon she left the girl's school she was

attending to enter a recently organized acting school that
would later be the Royal Academy of Dramatic Art. She
had not completed her course of studies there when she
found out that her father had died, that his estate was
small and would not support her in her studies, and that
her mother wanted her to return to the West Indies.
Rather than comply, she managed to find a job in the
chorus of a touring musical comedy that played the smaller cities of the north in winters and the lesser seaside
resorts in summers. This was not so much a professional
opportunity but a chance to eke out a bare survival (and
one even barer between tours). It was stultifying. "My
love and longing for books completely left me." It was an
education only on such subjects as the essential similarity
of different depressed industrial towns, or boiled onion
suppers, or cold rooms, or the strategems of grasping
landladies or stage-door gallants ("Swine, deary, swine,"
as the chorus girls agree in *Quartet*).

Even the limited lessons of this school of hard
knocks were not really learned. When a particularly
truculent gallery sent the young girl fleeing from the
stage, the manager soon fired her from the company.
"And what the hell are you doing on the stage, may I ask,
if you are frightened by an audience?" he wondered in
response to her explanation. Nevertheless, she persisted
in her desire to be a performer. Soon she was performing
in another arena where her prospects were no brighter. At
age nineteen she had entered into her first full affair with
an older man who would subsequently drop her but not
completely. She had an abortion and he, through an inter-
mediary, sent her money. The retrospective autobiographer can appreciate something of the complexity of this
situation: "It seems to me now that the whole business of
money and sex is mixed up with something very primitive
and deep. When you take money directly from someone
you love it becomes not money but a symbol. The bond is

now there. . . . 'I belong to this man, I want to belong to him completely.' It is at once humiliating and exciting." But the participant young woman was sunk mostly in torpor while waiting for his call. She would go on the same round of walks every day and then sleep "fifteen hours out of the twenty-four," sleep "as if dead." That state changed when the money changed. A regular check sent through a lawyer and requiring acknowledgment of receipt was not a symbol of love. It proved the affair was over. She wrote a short poem:

> I didn't know
> I didn't know
> I didn't know.

And "then [she] settled down to be miserable."

In the genesis of this misery we can also trace the genesis of a question that will continue to occupy Rhys as a writer. What, she asks in her novels, is the relationship between eros and economics, and, more specifically, how does the capitalization of beauty along with the stereotyped sex roles of western society (and particularly post-Victorian British society) impel women to embrace their own "commodityness"? In simpler terms, given the values of the time, what is the essential difference between a prostitute and a princess elevated to her new status by a storybook marriage? And if there is no essential difference, then what does the manifest social difference signify? Rhys suspects that if the Colonel's lady and Judy O'Grady are really, as folk wisdom would have it, sisters under the skin, then this similarity/difference tells us more about men than it does about women. Society blames the seduced and abandoned girl for her plight. She should have known better. But Rhys knows better than that. The whole process turned on more than the girl's gullibility. Anatomizing this first affair and others in the novels that she will later write, Rhys also anatomizes the society in which such affairs happen as a matter of course and the men who direct them along their standard course.

The end of this first affair also occasions Rhys's fumbling beginnings as a writer. Despondently surviving on the money paid to her after the relationship was over, Rhys allowed a chance female acquaintance to find her a "better" room. To dress up the new room, she bought some bright quill pens and several thick ledgers—something to put on a "bare and very ugly" table. That same night she felt compelled to set down her version of the affair—"everything that had happened to me in the last year and a half"—and wrote compulsively until she was done. She closed the account by noting, "Oh God, I'm only twenty and I'll have to go on living and living and living," and put the books away in a suitcase. For seven years she did not look at them again but during all that time she kept them with her.

For these seven years Rhys went on living much as before. Then, in 1917, she met, through Belgium refugee friends, Jean Lenglet who was temporarily in London on a diplomatic passport. Just before he had to return to Holland he asked her to marry him. She agreed. As soon as she could book passage after the war she sailed to Holland to join him, taking with her only a few clothes and the exercise books. The two were married and then moved to Paris, where she earned some money giving English lessons to children and he was, whenever asked, so "very vague about" his employment that "after a bit [she] stopped questioning him." In Paris the first baby was born and soon after died. Two years later, in 1922, a daughter, who survived, was born. And back in Paris, after living briefly in Vienna and Budapest while her husband was a secretary for the Interallied Disarmament Commission, Rhys finally took her next large step towards becoming a writer.

The two were, as was often the case, short of money. They decided that he would write a few articles; she would translate them into English and sell them to one of the English newspapers. Remembering that she had once met in London the wife of the *Times* correspondent in Paris, Rhys sought this woman out to see if she might be interested in helping Lenglet get published. Mrs. Adams happened to ask Rhys if she did any writing herself, and, told of the notebooks, asked if she could see them. Impressed by Jean Rhys's writing but not by Jean Lenglet's, this minor patron brought a much more influential patron onto the scene. She showed Rhys's somewhat revised journal to Ford Madox Ford, who was also impressed. Soon he was helping Rhys with her writing (at least to the degree of serving as a kind of an encouraging older and much more successful mentor).

Ford Madox Ford was himself one of the more intriguing figures in early twentieth-century British literature. During his long career he authored some forty novels, at least five of which are acknowledged masterpieces—the four-volume *Parade's End* series and *The Good Soldier* (his best novel and one of the major English novels of the twentieth century). Ford had been a close friend of Joseph Conrad and had even coauthored several books with Conrad. He was interested in the talent of younger writers and was willing to help them launch their own careers, publishing, for example, numerous new authors in *The Transatlantic Review*, which Ford edited during the twenties in Paris.[11] Rhys, too, was first published in this major literary magazine. Ford also had a propensity for becoming romantically involved with the younger women who came into his life. Indeed, at the time he met Rhys, he was living in Paris with Stella Bowen, a young Australian painter. But that fact did not stop him from presently living with Rhys too.[12]

The details of the unhappy involvement between Rhys and Ford will be more fully discussed in the chapter on *Quartet*, Rhys's fictionalized account of this part of her life. For the present it is enough to note that when Jean Lenglet was arrested in 1924 for currency offenses and for illegal entry into France and subsequently sentenced to prison, Ford and Bowen took Rhys in and generously supported her throughout part of a difficult time before Ford considerably added to her difficulties, first by entering into an affair with her and then by sending her away when the affair (conducted virtually under Bowen's nose) began to prove messy. But there were still benefits for Rhys. Through Ford she met other major literary figures such as James Joyce and Hemingway. Ford encouraged her, through example and advice, to polish her prose and refine her impressionistic style.[13] He published her first sketches and helped publish her first book, *The Left Bank*, for which he wrote the introduction. He arranged work for her both before and after the affair.[14] He continued to support her after the sexual relationship was over. He provided her, thanks to the affair, with the material for her first novel.

With Ford, as with her first affair, Rhys had some cause to suspect the fundamental unfairness of the relationship to which she had been a party. Once more the conventional view that she should have known better and that consequently her suffering was her own fault simply added insult to injury. And again she had no recourse but to write about it. In Amsterdam and trying at first to reestablish the marriage with her husband, she completed *Quartet* in 1927. But the rapprochement did not work. She left Jean Lenglet and Amsterdam for London, where she arranged for the publication of *Quartet* and met Leslie Tilden Smith, a publisher's reader with whom she began an affair and whom she married after divorcing Lenglet in 1932. Meeting and marrying Smith resulted in only a slightly more settled life than the one she had previously led. Living sometimes in Paris, sometimes in London, sometimes with her husband, and sometimes alone, Rhys continued her writing career, publishing *After Leaving Mr. Mackenzie* in 1930, *Voyage in the Dark* (reworked from those first notebooks) in 1934, and *Good Morning, Midnight* in 1939, just before the Second World War began.

Then Rhys disappeared from the public scene. She stopped writing. She had never been recognized during the thirties as a major author, and in a world preoccupied with war she found it easy, and perhaps tempting, simply to drop from sight. After her second husband died in 1945, she married his cousin, Max Hamer, and after he was arrested in 1952 for misappropriating company funds and imprisoned for six months, the two retired to rural Cornwall in 1953 and then in 1956 "to a small cottage outside a village in Devon" which remained Rhys's home until her death. Before that death, however, there were two more turns in her unlikely life and career. Sometime during the period of her long silence she began writing again and then in 1966 published her last novel, *Wide Sargasso Sea*, a book on which she had worked for some fifteen years and which was at once hailed as a classic. But even before that belated success Rhys had begun to be rediscovered. The BBC, broadcasting a radio dramatization of *Good Morning, Midnight* in 1958, appealed to the public for any information about the author. Jean Rhys wrote to identify herself. The broadcast, the knowledge that she was still alive, a few critics who remembered and wrote of the earlier novels all prompted a renewed interest in this author and her fiction, a process that was greatly accelerated by the success of *Wide Sargasso Sea* and that culminated in Rhys being praised by A. Alvarez in 1974 in the *New York Review of Books* as "quite simply, the best living English novelist."[15] So she lived to receive in her seventies and eighties the recognition and renown that had eluded her in her thirties and forties.

There is something satisfying in that belated fame, in

the fact that Rhys survived to garner the honors that definitely did not come when they were first due. It is gratify-
ing to see justice done, to see past injustice undone. Part
of the appeal lies, too, in the hope of anyone who labors
grossly unrewarded (and probably most of us think we
do) that "time will bear me out" and the proof that sometimes time does. But there is also something sad. Justice
delayed, the legal profession regularly reminds us, is justice denied. From this perspective, the attentions that
Rhys received at the very end of her life serve to
emphasize just how shabbily she was treated during most
of that life. How rewarding the honors and the money
might have been if they had come when she most needed
them—before disappointment registered too deeply.
Rhys observed in 1947: "If I stop writing my life will have
been an abject failure. It is that already to other people.
But it could be an abject failure to myself. I will not have
earned death."

Rhys's last act both to vindicate her "abject" life and
merit release from it was the writing of *Smile Please*. It is
not inappropriate that she died in the middle of that task,
nor is it surprising that intimations of mortality run
through the autobiography that describes most fully the
writer's childhood and then deals in a distinctly cursory
fashion with the different setbacks she suffered as an
adult.[16] But somehow, out of disappointments and disasters, came the novels, and out of long obscurity came
fame, whereupon, in her eighties, her health broken, the
author set out to set the record of her disordered past
straight. It is a life that revolves in an odd and even
idiosyncratically heroic circle. It is a life that also provides
a partial introduction to the fiction even though it in no
sense explains it. Rhys herself maintained that "all of a
writer that matters is in the book or books. It is idiotic to
be curious about the person." We do not have to fully
agree with her, but she is at least partly·right. It is the

novels that are most important, and it is to the novels that
I now turn.

2

Wide Sargasso Sea:
Remodeling the House of Fiction

A study of Jean Rhys's fiction can well begin with *Wide Sargasso Sea* which is commonly considered to be "her most powerful novel" and her one "masterpiece."[1] *Wide Sargasso Sea* is also Rhys's most socially important book. Certainly, it covers the most ground. A twentieth-century novel that tells the tragic story Charlotte Brontë omitted from her *Jane Eyre* and that grounds in the West Indies an inverted version of Brontë's nineteenth-century British fable of heroic selfhood, *Wide Sargasso Sea* necessarily conjoins in odd resonances the present century and the past one, the New world and the Old, slavery and freedom, triumph and defeat, incipient feminism (then and now) and the continuations of patriarchal prerogatives. Furthermore, this final novel particularly fits the writer's career as described in the previous chapter. With *Smile Please*, Rhys at the very end of her life wrote mostly about its beginnings. And with *Wide Sargasso Sea*, too, Rhys imaginatively returns to her own childhood and thoroughly grounds her last novel in the first reality that she knew, the West Indies. Starting with this same novel, we can start where she, as a writer, both ended and began.

Starting with *Wide Sargasso Sea*, we also almost necessarily start with *Jane Eyre*, but not for the reasons that have been suggested by critics such as Walter Allen who maintain that Rhys's novel does not "exist in its own right" since it requires Brontë's earlier text "to complement it, to supply its full meaning."[2] That whole argument of "dependency" is dubious. Many of Shakespeare's plays—plots, characters, and conclusion—are derived from somewhere else, but that consideration hardly brands the plays as derivative, and neither is James Joyce's *Ulysses* labeled a lesser, nonautonomous work because it leans so heavily on Homer's *Odyssey*. Nor are we ever told, to consider a somewhat lower and more parallel example, that William Golding's *Lord of the Flies* will yield up its "full meaning" (as if any major work of literature has only one "full meaning") only to readers who already know R. M. Ballantyne's *The Coral Island*, the nineteenth-century text inverted by Golding's twentieth-century one. There is, moreover, no crux of interpretation in *Wide Sargasso Sea* that can be resolved only through reference to *Jane Eyre*. The one novel can be read independently of the other just as Shakespeare's *Macbeth* can be viewed by an audience unversed in Holinshed's *Chronicle*.

This is not to argue for the irrelevance of the source. If one is going to analyze *Macbeth*, one might do well to start with Holinshed and consider what is changed and to what end. The same with *Wide Sargasso Sea* and *Jane Eyre*. Rhys's novel would still be a major work of literature even if Brontë's were somehow totally lost. But Brontë's novel is not lost and it does cast a certain light on Rhys's. Therefore (and to revive the memory of those readers who may have somewhat forgotten the novel) I will briefly review *Jane Eyre* and then note how Rhys both follows and inverts that earlier book. A comparison of the two novels also helps to clarify such matters as the function of particular scenes in the overall structure of *Wide Sargasso Sea*, the ways in which Rhys controls that structure, how she portrays her two main characters, and how those portrayals also portray the world these characters inhabit.

Jane Eyre, as even those who have not read the novel

generally know, is one of the most determined heroines in nineteenth-century literature. She is particularly determined not to settle for any of the lowly stations that life offers her but will, instead, make something of herself and will do so on her own terms, not society's (and particularly not those of the men in her society). Charlotte Brontë has her protagonist commence her progress through her various tribulations as a ten-year-old orphan tyrannized over by an aunt and her three children, all of whom treat Jane as an outcast. Rebelling against this family, the child is sent to Lowood School, a harsh orphanage for the daughters of indigent clergymen presided over by the hypocritical Mr. Brocklehurst. Prepared for the unprestigious position of governess, she next travels to Thornfield Hall, an isolated and faintly ominous country house, to take care of the education of the absent master's ward (probably his illegitimate daughter). At Thornfield, Jane contends with the various hints that something is wrong in the house and then with the problem of the returned master, Edward Rochester, who oozes Byronic angst and obviously carries a full charge of barely repressed sexual energy. Plain Jane succumbs reluctantly to the temptation to fall in love with such a masterful man but then resolutely resists Rochester's ploys to make her into either his mistress or his bigamous wife.

The fact of Rochester's previous marriage emerges even as the second ceremony is under way. The prospective bride learns that the former Bertha Mason of the West Indies, now Mrs. Rochester and mad, has been imprisoned all along on the third floor of Thornfield Hall. Jane flees to be taken in by a kindly family that coincidentally turns out to be her cousins, to discover through this new family that she is also an heiress, to resist the blandishments of the man in her new family that she join him in an asexual missionary marriage whereby they could both do good work among the heathens. Saved from that cold fate by a different supernatural calling, she hears Rochester's voice summoning her and returns to Thornfield to find that his house has been set on fire by Bertha. Rochester, blinded and crippled during his unsuccessful attempt to save his wife from the burning building, now resides in Fearndean, an old house deep in the woods. There Jane seeks him out; comforts him; and marries him, of course, to live in peace, harmony, and dignity. Two years later, after the birth of a son, Rochester even regains sight in one eye.

As numerous critics have pointed out, there is much more to *Jane Eyre* than its obviously romantic plot.[3] My concern, however, is not with the subtleties of Brontë's art, and I have summarized her novel on the simplest level in order to show that, on that same simplest level, Rhys's novel can be read as the story Brontë mostly glosses over. The first writer gives us only the sketchiest facts of the first marriage, briefly describing how Rochester was sent as a young man to the West Indies to make his fortune by marrying a Creole heiress, how he entered into marriage with a woman whom he barely knew and did not love, how he watched her go mad, and how he has dealt with her and conducted himself since. Rhys has observed that she was long haunted by the ghost of the mad first wife and, convinced that an English author had not done justice to that West Indian character, she determined to tell Bertha's real story.[4] In place of Rochester's brief retrospective account of the marriage, an account that even in *Jane Eyre* must be tinged with some self-justifying omissions or other flattering modifications, the reader is given the first wife's version of who and what she was prior to the marriage and then both versions of just how that marriage went wrong–a kind of his-and-her account of matrimonial disaster. As Rosalind Miles emphasizes, "Jean Rhys reminds us, as Charlotte does not, that a blasted and hopeless marriage happens to two people."[5] But perhaps

the most surprising feature of even a superficial assessment of *Wide Sargasso Sea* is the manner in which the later
book parallels the earlier one while also supplementing it
and inverts it while also paralleling it.

Sandra Gilbert and Susan Gubar in their general discussion of *Jane Eyre* in *The Madwoman in the Attic*
observe that the various other women characters in
Brontë's novel all serve to reflect the protagonist's predic-
aments. But Bertha, they point out, "is Jane's truest and
darkest double: she is the angry aspect of the orphan
child, the ferocious secret self Jane has been trying to re-
press ever since her days at Gateshead."[6] Rhys seizes, from
the beginning, on this aspect of the novel to show just
how much Jane's predecessor can be seen as another version of Jane. Antoinette Cosway, the protagonist in *Wide
Sargasso Sea* (who will later be named Bertha Mason) is
first portrayed as an even more abandoned "orphan" than
was Jane. The girl's father has died. The mother is left a
young woman without money or friends on an isolated,
decayed country estate where former slaves now jeer at
her poverty and threaten her life. The mother is also
preeminently concerned with a younger mentally defec-
tive son and has no time at all for her daughter. After that
son is killed in an abortive ex-slave uprising, the mother
even more repudiates the daughter and sinks into madness—what the daughter describes as "her death before her
death." At this point Antoinette is sent away to school, a
lax Catholic boarding school in place of Jane's overstrict
Protestant one, but a school that still shuts her away from
the world and does not prepare her for any real place in it.
Antoinette, even more than Jane, then leaves the school
to serve Rochester, to serve him directly and immediately
by marrying him and thus making him rich.

Rhys goes on in part 2 to have Rochester give his
own account of how he "played the part [he] was
expected to play" with his young bride and perhaps even
fell a little in love with her but soon fell out again; to have

Antoinette tell how she tried to win him back with an obeah (mild voodoo) love potion; to show how he viewed that act as an attempted poisoning and how the two contended at increasingly cold (on his part) and passionate (on hers) cross-purposes until both his implacable drive to dominate totally, and to justify to himself and her his exercise in tyranny, drive her mad. The novel ends some years later. He inherited his family estate in England and has returned there with his wife who is kept prisoner in the house. She dreams of burning down Thornfield Hall, an act that could serve as both a long-delayed revenge and a final bid for freedom. For Antoinette, only that last dream has any chance of coming true. The concluding sentences in the novel read: "Now at last I know why I was brought here and what I have to do. There must have been a draught for the flame flickered and I thought it was out. But I shielded it with my hand and it burned up again to light me along the dark passage."

The dark passage down which Antoinette walks alone to her death is, in the largest sense, the course of her entire life. That journey is carefully traced out in *Wide Sargasso Sea*. But the path Antoinette follows is also grounded in *Jane Eyre*. The earlier text "pre-scribes" the conclusion of the latter one and hence, by implication, the way to that conclusion. Jane's ultimate possession (of a fortune, of a family, of Rochester, of a life that fits her rigorous standards of what her life should be) is premised on Antoinette's ultimate dispossession (of her family, of her fortune, of Rochester, of any sense or possibility of directing her own life, of her sanity, of life itself). Moreover, Jane's final chief possession, Rochester, from whom her other goods flow, must necessarily be the main agent of Antoinette's terminal dispossession. To the degree that the earlier novel is the story of a woman coming into her own, the latter is the converse tale of a woman losing all she owned or ever hoped to have.

Just as Antoinette's final fate is pre-scribed by the

conclusion of *Jane Eyre*, so too is it prefigured by the beginning of *Wide Sargasso Sea*. In the first section of the novel the protagonist either retrospectively remembers or concomitantly reports her childhood on Coulibri, the ruined estate where she lived with her widowed young mother and mentally handicapped brother, and from the beginning ominous signs abound. Even the opening sentences of the novel register, for example, the isolated family's outcast status. From Martinique, the mother does not fit in with Jamaican society. Later, the daughter from Jamaica will not fit in when she is taken by her husband to England, a far more distant island. The mother's loneliness, the mother's grief, the mother's knowledge that youth and beauty have brought her to her sorry pass also anticipates—as does the similarity of their names, Annette and Antoinette—the daughter's fate. And still more specifically, the daughter's sense that she has been rejected by her mother and her awareness that she lives hated by the recently freed slaves who surround them (and who could, indeed, kill them all but find the prospect of the family's protracted poverty a better revenge) foreshadow a more devastating rejection and hatred to come.

The young girl still tries to see some kind of almost Eden in the wild grandeur of the ruined estate. "Our garden was large and beautiful as that garden in the Bible—the tree of life grew there. But it had gone wild, the paths were overgrown and a smell of dead flowers mixed with the fresh living smell." The fruit of the tree of life in this particular garden is mostly the knowledge of loss: "My father, visitors, horses, feeling safe in bed—all belonged to the past." In a real sense, she has been exiled from the garden while still remaining within it. As Ronnie Scharfman rightly observes, "Antoinette's childhood world, seen through any other eyes but her own, is already a paradise lost."[7]

Paradise is all the more lost in that for both mother

and daughter it briefly seemed that it might be regained. In both cases, too, the dashing of rekindled hope thematically and symbolically foreshadows the resolution of the novel. Yet the daughter's happiness with a childhood friend and the reason and the way in which that friendship is betrayed so subtly parallels Antoinette's subsequent treatment at the hands of Edward Rochester that it is easy to overlook the point of the earlier episode. The friend is Tia, a black girl who sometimes comes onto the estate. Swimming together in the river and adventuring in the forest almost every day, the daughter of a former slave-owner and the daughter of a former slave soon become close friends. For a time Antoinette escapes from her loneliness. Yet only for a time. The friendship ends with a childish quarrel but a quarrel replete with portentous implications.

A few pennies fall out of Antoinette's pocket as she and Tia are undressing to go swimming. Tia looks long at the coins and then bets Antoinette three of the pennies that she "couldn't turn a somersault under water 'like you say you can.'" Antoinette accepts the bet, turns the somersault, but is told that she "hadn't done it good" and that Tia has won. The two exchange words, Antoinette condemning Tia for her "cheating" and Tia condemning Antoinette for her poverty. After they part, Antoinette discovers that Tia has taken more than the money; she has also substituted her dirty, torn dress for Antoinette's only good one.

Briefly put, Tia's transgression against her friend is compounded because when she takes the cash, she wants the credit too. For her profiting to be justified in her own eyes, she must redefine the other party to the transaction. So Antoinette becomes a white nigger, and "black nigger better than white nigger," Tia claims, to claim also the right to resolve the disagreement between them as to whether Antoinette really did or did not turn her somersault. (The reader will note that there is as much metaphysical as physical somersaulting in this scene.) In that same vein, confiscating Antoinette's clean, starched dress constitutes another convenient exercise in symbolic redefinition. She, Tia, will be the deserving one, while Antoinette becomes the properly penniless ragamuffin. Later, with Rochester, Antoinette's three pennies will have grown into her thirty-thousand-pound dowry, but even though the stakes are then higher, the principle remains the same. Rochester not only takes all of Antoinette's money, he also insists that she must henceforth be "Bertha" (his name for her) and thereby, in one critics apt phrasing, "strips her of her individual essence."[8]

Antoinette returns home in her former friend's tattered dress to find unexpected company visiting her mother. The new owners of a nearby estate have come to call. Through these new neighbors the mother soon meets Mr. Mason, is courted by this wealthy young Englishman, marries him, and has a second chance at happiness. For a time all goes well. But the blacks resent the reestablished prosperity of the estate and fear Mason's plan, discussed before the servants, to replace the local workers with more tractable imported "coolies." The husband refuses to believe the wife's repeated warnings that trouble is brewing and remains to be caught, with his wife and her children, in a full-fledged ex-slave revolt. The house is fired; Pierre, Antoinette's handicapped brother, dies from the burns that he receives; the rest of the family escape with their lives only through a fortuitous accident of a pet parrot, its wings clipped, falling, burning, from the building. Local superstition holds "that it was very unlucky to kill a parrot, or even to see a parrot die." The crowd of rioters melts away; the surviving whites are left to cope with tragedy as best they can.

The chief victim of the tragedy is not, of course, the

husband who had insisted that the blacks were both too
lazy and too good-natured to pose any real danger, but
the wife who had been laughed at for her warnings and
told to "be reasonable." Confronting the immediate consequences of his reason–the estate destroyed, her son (the
favored child whom she perhaps loved more because of
his handicap) dead, her daughter almost dead–Annette
Mason not unreasonably gives way to grief and anger,
whereupon she suffers still another loss at the hands of
her husband. When after almost six weeks Antoinette
recovers consciousness, she remembers hearing, during
her illness, the "mother screaming . . . 'don't touch me.
I'll kill you if you touch me. Coward. Hypocrite. I'll kill
you.'" She is told that her mother is now
"resting" in the country, but the nature of the rest soon
becomes clear. Mr. Mason, perturbed by the violence of
his wife's rage, arranged to have the irrational woman put
away. As Phyllis Chesler in particular has argued, "mad
woman" is a category defined and applied by men, not by
women, and the definition typically serves those who
employ it.[9] The text doubly supports that contention.
Rochester, too, will presently find good reason for deciding his wife is mad.

   With the burning house lighting the sky and knowing that she will "never see Coulibri again"–"nothing
would be left, the golden ferns and the silver ferns, the
orchids . . . and the roses"–Antoinette still tries to save
something of her fast-vanishing already failed paradise.
She sees Tia among the rioters and "ran to her, for she was
all that was left of my life as it had been." The passage
continues: "As I ran, I thought, I will live with Tia and be
like her. Not to leave Coulibri. Not to go. Not. When I
was close I saw the jagged stone in her hand but I did not
see her throw it. I did not feel it either, only something
wet, running down my face." By putting out her arms to
the girl running towards her, Tia would acknowledge

friendship and consequently her own previous transgressions against · that friendship. She throws the stone instead.

Betrayal leads, here, to further betrayal, and violence against the other is also shown to be, in some sense, violence against the self. Thus the shock of double recognition with which this powerful scene ends: "I looked at her and I saw her face crumple up as she began to cry. We stared at each other, blood on my face, tears on hers. It was as if I saw myself. Like in a looking-glass." In the glass of the other each girl recognizes how little are the supposed differences between them and how little they can do about that recognition. The two are now sisters again but sisters in sorrow and suffering. And again Antoinette's present life anticipates her life to come. She and Rochester will finally be totally joined but only in desolation. In each case the burden of the tragedy is how easily it could have been a different sharing and how inevitably it was not.

At this point it is important to note that Antoinette's childhood tragedies are psychologically as well as symbolically related to her adult ones and that the author's control of this connection mitigates a common charge made against her. Rhys has been often criticized for portraying weak women who invite their tribulations by being much too dependent on the men in their lives.[10] "Why can't an Antoinette be more like a Jane?" is the question implicit in these critiques. But there is something dubious in that question, in the observation that it wouldn't have happened if. . . . The victim of a mugging, for example, might well be told that he should have been bigger, stronger, built like a football lineman. However, he is not likely to be consoled by that counsel, and, accurate as it may be, it is not particularly relevant to the mugging at hand. What I am arguing is that an understandable dissatisfaction with Rhys's psychologically frail protagonists (who definitely are not good role models) diverts the reader from considerations of how and to what end the central character, with all her frailties, is manipulated in the text.

Prefiguration, in *Wide Sargasso Sea*, is also predisposition. Antoinette's early suffering points the way to her later suffering and also makes that later suffering much more probable, which is to say that the different episodes run together thematically as well as structurally. For example, the quarrel with Tia early in the novel is all the more devastating because Antoinette knows her mother prefers the son, and that preference is immediately more painful to the young girl in that it has been validated by Tia's rejection of her, which is, in turn, revalidated by the mother. That night the daughter has a nightmare. She is awakened by the mother who comes not to comfort her but to tell her to be quiet. She is frightening Pierre. From such a shaky foundation it is hard to construct a firm sense of self, one that can stand up to a Rochester. Differently put, Rhys well knows that the weak are more likely to be victimized than the strong, and that the more they are victimized the weaker they become. It is hardly surprising, then, that essentially the same thing happens over and over again to the Rhys protagonist and that the text traces out the vicious circle in which this character is caught. Indeed, in Rhys's novels—to modify the equation at the beginning of this paragraph—chronology is typography.

Just as the bride's previous life, in *Wide Sargasso Sea*, almost foreordains a failed marriage, so too does the groom's. Clara Thomas rightly observes that "Rochester is as damaged by his father's failure to love him as Antoinette is by her mother's."[11] Seeing himself as a dispossessed and despised younger son, the new husband more than half suspects that despite the thirty-thousand-pound dowry already paid into his hands he is somehow being duped.[12] Furthermore, beautiful though his bride may be, she is clearly not a demure and proper English maiden. The setting of the honeymoon is strikingly picturesque but it could hardly look less like Britain. So what might be evidence of his great good fortune is also proof of his exiled state, and Rochester is from the first more ready to resent than to rejoice. The predisposition, indulged, soon flourishes. Burdened by their different pasts and their inability to understand each other's burden (or their own, for that matter), the newlyweds do not even make it through their honeymoon.

The marriage that begins badly and builds to devastating tragedy for both participants does so for thoroughly human reasons. In short, Rhys, in recasting Brontë's plot, refuses to make Rochester into simply the stock villain that he easily could have been. Yet Rochester, in *Wide Sargasso Sea*, does exactly what the stock villain would be called upon to do in any cautionary tale depicting the sad fate of a foolish maiden seduced into a thoroughly unsuitable marriage. He quickly convinces the girl that they should wed; as husband, he takes full control of all her property; once he has that control, he soon decides that he does not really love her and puts her aside in order to enjoy his new wealth on his own terms and with no disturbing recriminations. But the problem of interpreting this character is still more complicated in that there seem to be not two but three different Rochesters in the text. We have a psychologically disturbed man creating in the present different versions of his past traumas (and definitely in need of counseling, preferably of the "Can This Marriage be Saved" variety). We have the standard villain of sentimental fiction about whom women should be warned. And we also have the Byronic hero, for Rhys's Rochester always acts consistent with Brontë's, and at the end of *Wide Sargasso Sea* he has become precisely the same character whom Jane, in *Jane Eyre*, first meets at Thornfield Hall.

The subtlety of this three-sided portrayal centers especially in that third side. Essentially, Rhys's male lead ends up as a fully Byronic character wending, with cragged willfulness, his dark and solitary way through a world he holds in total contempt. Yet this last Rochester is portrayed in counterpoint to the other two, and that counterpointing penetrates the romantic mask. In effect, the three faces of Rochester reveal a pathetic man half caught in his final protective pose and half huddled behind it. The grand pose is thereby exposed as a convenient device for glossing over some distinctly petty actions. Rochester in the Byronic mode would never acknowledge how muddled he often is or admit to the mean actions that have sprung from his muddlement. *Wide Sargasso Sea*, however, undermines that stand by showing the confusions and self-deceptions at the heart of Rochester's heroic posturings.

The same point is made in somewhat different terms by Todd Bender who argues that Rhys "converts Rochester into a much more interesting, equivocal figure" than he was in *Jane Eyre* and thereby makes us "more aware of the limitations of Brontë's Rochester" and "of Jane's judgment."[13] Jane, after all, has her predecessor's fate before her. But in *Jane Eyre* the presence of the other woman is, as already noted, played down, and the first wife functions as the mostly hidden source of the novel's gothic trappings. Rhys transfers what we might term that watch-spring role from mad Bertha to sane Rochester. Indeed, one of the chief ironies in *Wide Sargasso Sea* is the way in which Antoinette's madness and also the final gothic conflagration both originate from Rochester's sanity—a sanity that is itself (these matters are always relative) a form of socially sanctioned madness.

"So it was all over," part 2 begins, as young Edward Rochester muses retrospectively about the brief preparations for the wedding ceremony just concluded. The newlyweds, embarked on their honeymoon, have stopped at a village on the way when a native woman who recognized Antoinette called out a greeting. The bride comes back to her husband waiting in the rain to say that the friend has asked them to take shelter in her house. He declines the invitation, noting that his new wife "spoke hesitantly as if she expected me to refuse, so it was easy to do so." More is at issue here than his unacknowledged racial prejudice or his early revealed propensity to fulfill Antoinette's worst expectations. The action, minor as it is, highlights the prophetic note in Rochester's first words. The marriage, too, is already almost "all over" even as it has barely begun.

Basically, Rochester has just been reflecting on how small a part he played in his own marriage–only one month in Jamaica "and for nearly three weeks of that time [he] was in bed with fever," yet already he is wed. He resents the manner in which he has been so expeditiously disposed of, a disposition he had actively pursued, but since he will not accept any of the blame himself, it must somehow be Antoinette's doing. He is also obviously pained at the way his own family has propelled him along on the course he has followed. "Dear Father," runs the letter that he composes in his head as he and Antoinette ride on after he has refused the invitation to stop. "The thirty thousand pounds have been paid to me without question or condition. . . . I have a modest competence now. I will never be a disgrace to you or to my dear brother the son you love. No begging letters, no mean requests. None of the furtive shabby manoeuvers of a younger son. I have sold my soul or you have sold it." One present shabby manoeuver (selling himself) will preclude others (begging in the future for family support). He is understandably angry with this choice of disgraces, and the anger that he, an insignificant younger son, cannot lay at his father's distant doorstep is readily transferred to the new wife conveniently at hand. Moreover, he intends to counter his poor-relative role in his previous family by his different higher status in his present one. Finally, these three factors are all magnified by a fourth one, Rochester's understandable desire to believe that the fortune now totally in his hands has ended up just where it belongs. He will be the deserving one; she must be somehow subservient and properly dispossessed; otherwise he has simply defrauded her.

With Rochester, family politics, sexual politics, colonial politics ("Why can't these islanders be more English?"), and economic politics all run confusedly together. In each case, he is so caught up in the role he thinks he plays that he does not at all examine the role he actually plays. And those discrepancies that he does recognize are immediately discounted; thus his excuse to himself for treating Antoinette and her friend so rudely during the brief honeymoon stop: "'Well,' I thought. 'I have had fever and am not myself yet.'" But he *is* himself all along, a man afflicted with what Peter Wolfe aptly terms a "pawn complex" who, in his determination to deny his supposed subservient status, almost innocently treats all those around him in the intolerable fashion that— as he never notices—no one is treating him. [14] Consider, for example, his insistence that "I have not bought her, she has bought me, or so she thinks." Who said anything about anybody buying anybody? Certainly not Antoinette. But he casts the marriage into purely material terms (his terms, not hers) and then denies his own self-defined status of purchased husband by insisting, even as he pockets the cash, that he remains his own man. Her imputed motives in a transaction in which she had no voice justify his behavior. [15] Keeping her money will show her that she cannot buy a man like him.

Rochester's "pawn complex" largely precludes any possibility of living happily with Antoinette, and his different declarations of independence soon finish off the faltering union. These begin with the honeymoon journey scene previously discussed but include still other actions such as his trampling the wedding wreath he is given at the end of that journey or his making love to Amélie, Antoinette's impertinent servant, while Antoinette listens in the next room. It is that last and most despicable action that terminates any pretense of a real marriage and leaves the new wife raging, hating, ready to be pushed into permanent madness. Yet even at his worst, Rochester, Rhys shows, still has understandable albeit characteristically confused and twisted reasons for acting as he does.

The devastating affair is, of course, prima facie proof that Rochester has not been purchased as a man, that he will bestow his favors where he pleases, so to speak. It is also the consequence of the contradiction between this character's sexuality and his proto-Victorian views regarding the proper forms of sexuality. The problem is not just the powerful physical passion that he feels for the woman whom he would prefer to hold at a certain emotional distance and the consideration that such passion in a man committed to complete self-control must engender a certain "self-revulsion."[16] The problem is also *her* passion. Rhys makes Rochester a thoroughly nineteenth-century man who well knows what his bride's amorous inclinations should be. He is allowed an unfortunate but necessary depravity (the species, after all, must be propagated). She is not, for it is her proper asexual demureness that channels, limits, and even licenses his licentiousness. Her sacrifice almost redeems his sin. Such, then, were the rules of the game. For her to take pleasure in the transaction would be depraved, unnatural, something that only a prostitute or a madwoman might do.

Yet the physical lovemaking is pleasurable and perhaps all the more pleasurable in that the pleasure is definitely mutual. It is a dangerous impasse for this would-be moral man, and particularly dangerous in that Rhys's Rochester, as much as Brontë's, is charged with sexual energy. But Rhys, more than Brontë, knows how dangerous both the suppression and the expression of socially skewed sexual impulses can be. Rochester at one point asks himself, "I wonder if she [Antoinette] ever guessed how near she came to dying. . . . It was not a safe game to play—in that place. . . . Death came very close in the darkness."

A different death soon arrives in a different darkness. Rochester is rescued from his sexual and moral impasse by the fortuitous arrival of a letter from an unknown correspondent. Daniel Cosway, an embittered black man, expresses at length and in convoluted terms his moral outrage at how Rochester has been "shamefully deceived by the Mason family." Cosway claims that the Masons have profited from the newcomer's ignorance and innocence to foist off on him a wife tainted by family insanity and already going the way of her wicked, mad mother. There are, of course, some questions that this letter well might prompt. Why did the man who proclaims that he is acting out of "Christian duty" wait, as Cosway admits he waited, until the letter comes too late to do anything but cause grief, when a more timely warning would have easily forestalled the unfortunate marriage? And even more pointedly, how does that "Christian duty" (the Lord looms large in Cosway's letter) soon devolve into a crude attempt at blackmail? Is a Christian doing his duty owed, as Cosway presently suggests, five hundred pounds for his services and his silence? Rochester, however, entertains no such reservations. The letter tells him exactly what he already wants to believe: "It was as if I'd expected it, been waiting for it."

Cosway effectively weaves a number of known truths into his damning portrayal of the woman whom he also claims as a half-sister. Yet the validity of the various charges and particularly the suggestion of Antoinette's previous promiscuity (for which no evidence is adduced) is never really the issue. Rhys calculatingly plays off what Rochester later remembers ("*Give my sister your wife a kiss for me. Love her as I did—oh yes I did.*") against what Cosway actually said when Rochester visited him ("Give my love to your wife—my sister. . . . You are not the first to kiss her pretty face") to show how the husband's mind runs on this matter. Even the disgusting Cosway becomes, for Rochester, one of Antoinette's former lovers and an incestuous lover at that. What we see here is a man embracing his own imagined betrayals. After such knowledge, what forgiveness? Compared to her past actions, his small present slip with Amélie, "so gay, so natural," merits "not one moment of remorse." And justified hypocrite that he is, he can injure his bride in a far more devastating fashion than he himself would be injured were all of Cosway's insinuations true.[17]

Rochester, however, is twice brought to at least a partial confrontation with his own behavior. The first is forced by Christophine, Antoinette's childhood nurse and the one person who cared for her when she lived at Coulibri. After the fiasco with Amélie, Antoinette takes refuge with Christophine, who soon charges Rochester with just what he has done. "It was like that, I thought. It was like that," he can acknowledge as Christophine points out how "you marry her for her money and you take it all. And then you want to break her up, because you jealous of her"; how "you pretend to believe all the lies that dam bastard tell you" and "you meant her to hear" you with that "worthless girl." Christophine also knows how full of hate Daniel is and that it was the treatment of Antoinette's mother—at the permanent sexual disposal of a man into whose care she was put—that has driven her mad.

Christophine's intent is to see if there is any possibility of reviving love between the two (she knows that

Antoinette would be more than willing) or, failing that, to have Rochester settle at least a portion of the dowry on Antoinette and leave her in Christophine's care. Yet Rochester will not indulge any dawning intimations of responsibility. At the first hint of money, the "dazed, tired" man was suddenly "alert and wary, ready to defend [him]self." That reaction gives his true concern away. Someone is after his cash. At once a victim again, he can "blame" Christophine "for all that has happened here." She provided Antoinette with the love potion which was given to him and which was, he declares, poison (even though he did not die), while the rum Christophine administered to the distraught girl was, Rochester claims, simply to make her drunk, out of "hatred of me I suppose." He can now laugh at the "ridiculous old woman" and threaten her with the police.

Rochester's second chance to recognize and rise above the disaster that he is precipitating for himself as well as for Antoinette comes as they are preparing to leave Granbois, the site of the abortive honeymoon. Reviewing his brief stay at the estate, he juxtaposes bits of what Christophine said with what Daniel said or what he himself has presumed and thereby also juxtaposes the fleeting pleasure of his recent past with the enduring pain of what he sees as a foredoomed and inescapable future. *"She love you so much, so much. She thirsty for you. Love her a little like she say"* is shortly followed by "She thirsts for *anyone*—not for me" and "She'll moan and cry and give herself as no sane woman would—or could."[18] But into this pleasant exercise in envisioned martyrdom ("Pity. Is there none for me? Tied to a lunatic for life—a drunken lying lunatic—gone her mother's way") a strangely different thought intrudes. "Suddenly, bewilderingly, I was certain that everything I had imagined to be truth was false. False. Only the magic and the dream are true—all the rest's a lie. Let it go. Here is the secret. Here."

It is his one intimation that his insistence on proper

English behavior in all matters from the most public (claiming the dowry) to the most private (going to bed) is, in a beautiful and very un-English Far Antilles setting, all one vast and self-perpetrated fraud. He also suspects that he himself may be his chief victim. Stories of pirate treasure that Antoinette previously recounted suddenly run through his mind as a metaphor for his dawning recognition. "The law of treasure" is to find it first and then to guard it well. The thirty thousand pounds with which he has been totally preoccupied has blinded him to the two real treasures that, quite unnoticed, he is on the verge of forfeiting—his wife and his integrity. For it is not just Antoinette whom he is throwing away; as Michael Thorpe observes, Rochester "violates his own soul in destroying [hers]."[19]

The pirates too become a metaphor for the dimly perceived "secret treasure" and the consequent choice on the brink of which he stands. He and Antoinette will hear again the heartstopping song of the mountain bird and "see the Emerald Drop, the green flash [of the setting West Indies sun] that brings good fortune." She "must laugh and chatter as [she] used to do—telling me about the battle off the Saints. . . . Or the pirates and what they did between voyages. For every voyage might be their last." That final thought of living fully in the face of unpredictable fortune and imminent death almost changes Rochester into an existentialist before his time. "Like the swaggering pirates, let's make the most and best and worst of what we have. Give not one-third but everything. All—all—all. Keep nothing back. . . ."

He doesn't make it. The closest he comes is to proclaim his recognition: "I have made a terrible mistake. Forgive me." But even as he voices his apology and plea, they both vanish, "Seeing the hatred in her eyes" as he spoke, he also instantly feels "my own hate spring up to meet" hers. The man who had no trouble returning his animosity for her love cannot bear to have that exchange reversed. If it is hatred she wants, he, in effect, says, it will be hatred that she gets, and he will be better at that game than she is: "We'll see who hates best. . . . My hate is colder, stronger, and you'll have no hate to warm yourself. You will have nothing." If it is hatred that she wants, even that shall be taken from her, because—as this sudden change that is really no change at all attests—it is hatred that he wants. And his metaphor of the pirates undergoes an about-face. Instead of giving everything, he will take everything; instead of pirate as independent existentialist, we have pirate as thoroughgoing thief who totally denudes his victim for the pleasure of demonstrating that he has the right and the power to do so.

In complete control again, freed of "all the mad conflicting emotions . . . wearied and empty" and most of all "sane," it is somehow Rochester who, despite his abundance of hatred, has forfeited everything: "I hated the mountains and the hills, the rivers and the rain. I hated the sunsets of whatever color. I hated its beauty and its magic and the secret I would never know." But "above all I hated her. For she belonged to the magic and the loveliness. She had left me thirsty and all my life would be thirst and longing for what I had lost before I found it."

He realizes that his instant switch from love to hate will not be itself reversed. Rhys emphasizes the pathos of that recognition by providing a subsidiary "chorus" character who perfectly sums up Rochester's plight. The scene ends with a small boy, told earlier that he could go away with the master and told now that he cannot, weeping inconsolably. The long middle section of the novel concludes with Rochester asking himself, "Who would have thought that any boy could cry like that. For nothing. Nothing. . . ." Yet it requires no great perspicacity to see that this dispossessed, disconsolate, lost little boy is a stand-in for Rochester himself; is, indeed, the Rochester whom that same character, with his pose of domination and control, would hide from all eyes, especially his own, and, as such, the child weeps for everything, everything.

Other possibilities hover in the background of the long second section. Rochester could have listened more to Christophine and less to Daniel Cosway; he might have made that existential breakthrough and renounced his contorted claiming of her cash; he should have seen how much Antoinette outweighed her dowry–that she was the treasure that eluded him to the very degree that he insisted on having her firmly in his grasp. And Antoinette, too, had other options; the denouement is not just of Rochester's making. Her capable Aunt Cora (the woman who earlier saved the family when Coulibri was burned and then nursed Antoinette back to health) advised the niece not to marry Rochester on any terms. At the last moment Antoinette sensed his ambivalent feelings and called off the wedding, but then let herself be convinced by his promises of "peace, happiness, and safety" that he loved her (whereas he was really mostly concerned with how he would look "going back to England in the role of rejected suitor"). Christophine tells her, once the marriage has begun to sour, that "woman must have spunks to live in this wicked world" and that she should simply leave him. When Antoinette admits that she cannot do that, Christophine then advises her to "ask him pretty for some of your own money" and go to another island; "stay away, ask more"; when he finally comes and "see you fat and happy he want you back."

In contrast to part 2, however, the brief final section moves directly and almost inevitably to the novel's tragic conclusion. This is partly because Rhys, who has already fully differentiated her story from Brontë's, must also accommodate the delimiting parallels. "After the power and the passion of Part II," Clara Thomas observes, "Part

III locks *Wide Sargasso Sea* into the final action of *Jane Eyre*."[20] Thornfield Hall must burn; Bertha Mason must die in the blaze that she set. In the last sentences of Rhys's novel, Antoinette/Bertha is preparing to light the fire she has just dreamed. But even here, as Antoinette earlier insisted in *Wide Sargasso Sea*, "there is always the other side, always." For Brontë, the full and final demonstration of Bertha's madness is her flaming suicide. For Rhys, that same fate is Antoinette's most decisive action and her final escape from further domination. Ironically, in *Wide Sargasso Sea*, the dispossessed madwoman acting out a mad dream does considerably better by herself than did the same woman sane and endowed with a fortune and pursuing the standard dream of love, marriage, and happiness ever after. That difference, Rhys suggests, signifies more about woman's reality than woman's insanity.[21]

In other words, there is a certain logic in Antoinette's madness and particularly in the last act inspired by that madness. "The only gesture of self-assertion which is left to her once she has been transported to England and relegated to being the mad woman in the attic, is one of self-immolation."[22] That suicide demonstrates that Rochester "does not destroy her. He does not even reduce her to the pitiful depraved creature we see in Antoinette's mad mother."[23] There is also a certain justice and symmetry in Antoinette's final action. Since Rochester early robbed her of her island heritage, she will finally deprive him of part of his. Indeed, by burning Thornfield Hall, the ancestral manor that he inherited and returned to soon after he had established himself in the West Indies, she hits him where it will most hurt, in his quintessential Englishness.

The dream of burning is more difficult to interpret than is the action it precedes, as even a few passages can attest: "I . . . saw the sky. It was red and all my life was in it. I saw the grandfather clock and Aunt Cora's patchwork, all colours, I saw the orchids and the stephanotis and the jasmine and the tree of life in flames." Or even more problematic: "Tia was there. She beckoned to me and when I hesitated, she laughed. I heard her say, You frightened? . . . Someone screamed and I thought, *Why did I scream*? I called 'Tia!' and jumped and woke." As Ronnie Scharfman observes, this "retrospective and reflective" vision of a world in flames "recreates and repeats the destruction of [the protagonist's] childhood world."[24] Antoinette thereby undoes what others did to her by becoming herself mistress of the conflagration. Mary Lou Emery has more recently carried similar considerations still further. "In the dream," Emery argues, "Antoinette creates the self that others have denied her" even as she also "condenses . . . all the private images of her inner life and the conflicts of her social world."[25] This dream allows her the power "to act where she actually is— in the midst of two worlds and in a new fictional reality, in the wide Sargasso Sea that dissolves Victorian distinctions between public and private experience, legitimate and illegitimate sexuality, madness and reason, primitive and civilized behavior, fiction and fact."[26]

Only a few other points need be added to this persuasive assessment of the conclusion of the novel. I have already observed how effectively Antoinette's early misfortunes prefigure larger disasters yet to come. But just as effectively, the last of those disasters, the impending loss of life itself, reflects back to the first great loss, the destruction of Coulibri. This conjunction of the first and the final fire especially serves to define the shape of Antoinette's experience as a cycle of disasters that, given circular form, can spin beyond the novel's end. The nineteenth-century fable continues on into its twentieth-century retelling and, of course, beyond. In this same respect, we can note how calculatingly Rhys places her protagonist's death. At the end of the novel, it is yet to come, it is there just beyond the last sentences, which is another way of continuing the text even though it has ostensibly concluded.

The conjunction of the two fires also highlights, as both Scharfman and Emery suggest, one of Rhys's main thematic concerns. The first destruction is a belated ex-slave revolt; the second might well be described as a belated ex-wife revolt. Each is an essentially irrational and ultimately ineffectual lashing out at a posited inferior status which can ostensibly justify that status—see, those blacks are brutes; look, that woman is mad—but which better suggests that the proof of "inferiority" is produced by being enforced from above. Thus the blacks who would kill Mason and his family have been brutalized by the recently abolished official slavery and the still continuing unofficial one. Or Rochester, closely guarding his shameless wife even on the ship to England, brings her to throw herself at the cabin boy, provocatively imploring him to help her escape, and thereby acting in precisely the depraved manner she was imprisoned to prevent. So, as Rhys insists, the standard structures of power with their attendant distinctions do not hold. Brutality can better be ascribed to the slave-holder than to the slave who has no choice in the matter. Neither does their posited superiority protect those supposedly situated on high. Rochester is as much the prisoner of the customs of his country and the assumptions of his class as Antoinette is the prisoner of Rochester. It is his insistence that *he* will not be a deceived husband that makes him one.

Rhys knows how arbitrary are the distinctions of power, be they based on race, class, or gender. But in the final dream only some of these distinctions collapse. Christophine again helps Antoinette, and Tia now beckons to her, but Rochester remains out of sight, present only as the voice (how appropriate) of "the man who hated me." Obviously all arbitrary distinctions are not created equal. In the present time of her imminent death, Antoinette can imaginatively bridge differences in class and race and thereby abolish the twisted consequences of those differences in action in the past (for example, Tia throwing the stone). Yet one old abyss looms as large as ever. She can envision the sisterhood of woman and woman but not the "brotherhood," the "siblinghood"– we do not even have a word for it yet–of woman and man.[27]

A classic, T. S. Eliot points out in his famous essay "Tradition and the Individual Talent," is a work that alters the way we view other works.[28] By this definition, *Wide Sargasso Sea* must be deemed a classic, and not just because, as Todd Bender points out, "after reading *Wide Sargasso Sea* we can never again read *Jane Eyre* with the same acquiescent acceptance of the animality of the confined wife, the perfection of manliness in Rochester, and the justice of the Englishwoman's claim to supersede the vile West Indian."[29] Rhys, with her best novel, requires that we read any and all romances differently–whether they be of the lower Harlequin variety or of considerably greater stature–novels such as Samuel Richardson's *Pamela*, Jane Austen's *Pride and Prejudice* or *Emma*, or Charlotte Brontë's *Jane Eyre* (even if there were no connections between that work and *Wide Sargasso Sea*). To the very degree that a romance builds to the standard fairy-tale conclusion–"and they were married and lived happily ever after"–it is undone by Rhys's weighing of the "happiness" and the "after." In this sense, as Gilbert and Gubar observe, *Wide Sargasso Sea* completes *Jane Eyre* as much as it anticipates it, for Antoinette and Edward begin approximately where Jane and Rochester end, married and with certain chasms (personal, social, cultural) to be bridged over by their lives together.[30] Romances posit bridges, conjunctions. Rhys returns us to the chasms.

Wide Sargasso Sea is a classic in a still larger sense too. "I did not even know her," Rochester observes of Bertha at one point in *Jane Eyre*. Rhys knows how truly he then spoke and how much he speaks for all of us. Indeed, the earlier novel is premised on nobody–neither its author, nor its characters, nor its readers–knowing Bertha. And again *Jane Eyre*, as reflected through *Wide Sargasso Sea*, is paradigmatic. We need to be reminded how much the story that is there supersedes and suppresses other possible stories implicit in that first one. The story most missing is usually a woman's story, and is so much "not there" that we typically do not even notice its absence. Yet imagine what Rhys might have done had she rewritten other classics of English literature, say "Dora Copperfield" or "Portrait of the Artist as the Young Woman." Essentially, then, I am arguing that *Wide Sargasso Sea* is a great novel for several reasons, for its psychological and structural complexity and for its social implications. Of all of Rhys's novels it most calls into question the patriarchal bias implicit in much modern western literature.[31] As Mary Lou Emery points out, all of "Rhys's heroines" employ the "privileged vision of exile" both to "expose sexual and cultural domination" and to "resist [that] domination."[32] But it is Antoinette saying "no" in fire who most clearly speaks the privileged vision of these exiles.

3

Voyage in the Dark:
The Early Tragedies of the Rhys Protagonist

The first four novels stand somewhat apart from the final one and not just because of the twenty-seven year silence that preceded the publication of that last novel. As even their titles might suggest, *Quartet*, *After Leaving Mr. Mackenzie*, *Voyage in the Dark*, and *Good Morning, Midnight* are all somewhat narrower in vision and design than is *Wide Sargasso Sea*. They are grounded in the limits of the author's own life, not in her transcending the limitations of another writer's imagination. Portraying contemporaneous protagonists—women down and almost out in Paris and London—these substantially autobiographical novels do not evince the larger resonances of *Wide Sargasso Sea*, with its juxtaposition of romance and reality, its casting of the whole envisioned world as wilful dream and/or gross misrepresentation.

Unlike *Wide Sargasso Sea* which was, in the sixties, immediately hailed as a classic, the other novels were, when published in the twenties and thirties, little noted and soon forgotten. This difference, however, does not so much mark a difference in the texts as in the times. The fact that the earlier works are now all in print, widely read, and generally praised represents another case of the public's taste finally catching up to the artist's accomplishment. And even if the first novels were not masterpieces before their time—like Emily Brontë's

Wuthering Heights or Herman Melville's *Moby Dick*—
they are still major works by a major writer and as such
deserve our attention. Indeed, we are only now beginning
to see just how well Rhys wrote even at the beginning of
her career. [1]

There is another obvious difference between the
early works and the last one. It is tempting to arrange the
four partly biographical fictions "in order of their internal
chronology [and] find in them one, fairly sequential
story," but it is a temptation that, as I will subsequently
argue, is "better resisted."[2] Yet the first novels do present
a generalized character (often referred to as the Rhys protagonist) at four different stages in her life. *Voyage in the
Dark* gives us the first stage. This third novel portrays a
protagonist's initial encounters with European (more
specifically, English) manners and mores and her first
grapplings with the problems of maturity, particularly
the intertwined and, for the Rhys heroine, most difficult
questions of how she will earn her living and how she will
cope with her own developing sexuality. The book also
most graphically shows how badly the young protagonist
will mismanage her life and so is paradigmatic for the
other studies of older women who fare no better.

Voyage in the Dark can seem, on first reading, to be
little more than a simple, cautionary tale. The work portrays a character who progresses, in a phrase from Saul
Bellow's *Herzog*, "from humble beginnings to complete
disaster." We first encounter Anna Morgan at age eight-
een and recently arrived in England from the West Indies.
Her father, a not particularly successful island planter,
has died. His second wife, Anna's stepmother, whom the
widower father married during the course of an earlier
business trip to London, has sold what was left of her
husband's West Indies estate and returned to England,
bringing Anna with her. The young woman soon realizes
that she is expected to support herself and at first does so

by performing in a traveling music troupe. It is, despite the ostensible glamor of the stage, a gray, grim life: "You were perpetually moving to another place which was perpetually the same. There was always a little grey street leading to the stage-door of the theatre and another little grey street where your lodgings were, and rows of little houses with chimneys like thé funnels of dummy steamers." To escape a life that, like those dummy steamers, is going nowhere, Anna early allows herself to be picked up by an obviously well-to-do older man, Walter Jeffries.

The escape goes nowhere too. More accurately, it takes her down instead of up, and the early image of the fake steamships slides into a recurring imagery of drowning that suggests, as Louis James observes, "spiritual death."[3] When she is presently dropped by Walter, Anna drifts into other affairs and then into casual prostitution. Near the end of the novel she is pregnant and almost penniless. Called on in this emergency, her first lover provides some cash to pay for an abortion. Rhys originally intended to conclude the novel with Anna dying after a botched abortion. But her publisher insisted that such an ending would be too pessimistic, so the author provided another conclusion no less despairing—Anna surviving: "She'll be all right,' he [the attending doctor] said. 'Ready to start all over again in no time, I've no doubt.'" The callousness of his prognosis registers on the young woman: "When their voices stopped the ray of light came in again under the door like the last thrust of remembering before everything is blotted out. I lay and watched it and thought about starting all over again. And about being new and fresh. And about mornings, and misty days, when anything might happen. And about starting all over again, all over again. . . ." (ellipsis in the original). That light glimmering under the doorway like the last flickerings of expiring consciousness presages, as Anna well knows, no rosy dawn nor new, fresh beginning.

The final ellipsis does not trail off, then, into indeterminacy. On the contrary, it quite accurately forecasts the protagonist's future, which must be, at best (i.e., "starting all over again"), simply another version of her recent past.[4] Thus the ending returns us to the novel itself; to Walter, whom Anna loved; to Carl Redman, who succeeded Walter and whom she tried to admire; to the nameless man who succeeded Carl and who impregnated her; to the even more unknown man—"He had a little close-clipped moustache and one wrist was bandaged. Why was it bandaged? I don't know. I didn't ask"—who was with her when she realized that she was pregnant; to the men who will come after these men once Anna is recovered and on the street again. That progression defines the increasingly narrow parameters of her life. Much more can be expected from the first man than the third. What she gets from the third man is, in fact, the pregnancy that almost kills her. But Rhys, in charting her protagonist's fall, does not at all provide an admonitory delineation of the consequences of woman's sexual sin.

The seduction novel is, of course, typically characterized by the conventional bias of its moralistic import.[5] The hero may occasionally slip into the wrong bed but the heroine never. Indeed, the rewarding of female virtue and the punishing of female vice—vice and virtue both defined only in the narrowest sexual terms—have been staples of English fiction from its inception. Thus Samuel Richardson's *Pamela*, published in 1749 and commonly regarded as the first British novel, portrays a protagonist whose chastity is tested by the various blandishments and stratagems of her amorous, if inept, employer, Squire B. All his attempts foiled, the squire finally decides to marry the girl, thereby elevating the former maid to ladyhood. In contrast to *Pamela*, Richardson's subsequent novel *Clarissa* basically portrays the fatal consequences of even a forced fall from virtue. Literally thousands of subsequent works have preached one side or the other (and often both) of the same moralistic message. For Rhys, however, it is all claptrap. As she has one of her characters observe, early in *Voyage in the Dark*, "I bet you a man writing a book about a tart tells a lot of lies one way and another."

Rhys does not deny the disastrous state into which the fallen woman easily declines. The prostitute with the heart of gold who earns and keeps (she has, after all, had lots of practice) the love of a good man is another wish-fulfillment definition of women designed by and for men. Rhys admits the "wages of sin." What she refuses to admit is the significance commonly ascribed to those wages. They represent not a woman's appropriate reward but her impressed labor. They do not characterize the female employee; they characterize her male employer. In short, by simply shifting the moral focus of the standard seduction novel, Rhys effectively presents some tart truths of her own, and her tartest is her demonstration that Anna fell as much when she was taken to England by her stepmother as when she was taken to bed by Walter.

The book "about a tart" referred to in *Voyage in the Dark* is Emile Zola's *Nana*. It is not fortuitous that the two names, Nana and Anna, are almost identical. As A. Alvarez observes, early in the novel the young "virgin chorus girl is reading 'Nana'; at the end she, like Nana, is on the game, but chillingly and without any of Zola's unearned polemic."[6] This is accurate so far as it goes. However, and as Helen Nebeker rightly emphasizes, Rhys's main point surely lies more in the differences between the two women than in the identity of their profession. Nana, Nebeker points out, is "conniving, greedy, mindless, utterly evil in Zola's treatment"; she "brings destruction upon many men," but "in the end . . . justice triumphs: her sins are punished," and "she dies a horrible death from small pox."[7] We see in Zola the same old seduction-tale morality with a vengeance. In contrast, "Rhys, comprehending the shallowness of Zola's sentimental, didactic prejudices, employs this male 'morality play' of another time, another place to enhance the stark realism of her emerging female truth."[8] This truth need not be, as Nebeker extensively argues, that woman's original natural goddess status has been taken from her by man. The deprivation, I would maintain, occurs on a somewhat lower level. Rhys portrays a society in which women—particularly marginal women—are robbed of their status as full human beings and in which that robbery is so "natural" that it is hardly ever even reported.

From the first Anna is portrayed as a woman more sinned against than sinning. Her fate is seen as a result of her youth and inexperience and the way those qualities are used against her. Coming to England as a young woman, she simply does not kow how that island, so radically different from her warm childhood island, works. But she soon finds how her new world turns. In cold, dark, gray, frightening London, Anna is ripe only for the taking, and taken she is. And not just sexually. Early in the novel much of the first money that Walter gives her goes for a too expensive dress that does not quite fit but which is, the shop owner assures Anna, "perfect." When, disconsolate after Walter has abandoned her, she is rented a room by an older woman, Ethel Matthews, she never noticed how that ostensible act of charity is intended to provide some window dressing for and even a possible partner in Ethel's massage business. Nor does she notice how much that business verges towards a much older one and neither does she demur when Ethel soon raises the rent. Near the end of the novel, just before she desperately needs cash for an abortion, she "lends" a considerable sum to a former music-hall friend trying to make herself a little more presentable for a man whom this aging chorine hopes to marry. We see Anna as gullible and overgenerous and simply unable to cope. No match for even a saleslady, she can hardly be expected to resist Walter's more devious pitch.

Rhys also requires the reader to note how and why Anna faces her various challenges alone. One of the more poignant scenes in the book is the young protagonist's single meeting with her stepmother. This encounter takes place a few months after Anna has left the theatrical company to remain in London with Walter. Hester, the stepmother, has heard rumors that the girl is "beginning to turn out badly" but meets with her not to offer help or even any motherly counsel: "Don't imagine that I don't guess how you're going on. Only some things must be ignored some things I refuse to be mixed up with I refuse to think about even." Hester wants merely to voice her own outrage at the "plain speaking" of another family member. She has written to Anna's uncle in the West Indies, offering to pay half the girl's return fare, since "life in England" is not "agreeing with her very well." The uncle, in his lengthy response, insists that he will not have the penniless girl foisted onto him, that he will take Anna in only if she comes back with "her proper share of the money you [Hester] got from the sale of her father's estate. Anything else would be iniquitous—iniquitous is the only word." After she callously reads the Uncle's letter aloud to the unwanted girl, Hester goes on to assert that she has already done more than anyone could expect her to do for her stepdaughter: "I paid your expenses and your doctor's bill when you were ill in Newcastle and that time you had a tooth stopped I paid that too," and "I'll always be glad to do what I can for you. But if it's a question of money, please remember that I've already done far more than I can afford." The uncle had claimed that the father intended the money from his estate to go to his daughter. Hester vehemently counters that her "conscience is quite clear," her vehemence suggesting that perhaps it is not. What is clear, however, is that so far as

Anna is concerned her family is quite happy to throw her to the wolves.

The wolves are just as happy to catch her. In another way too, Anna is caught largely because of her unfortunate family situation. The novel gives no definite dates, but it is clear that Anna's mother died considerably before her father did. The girl rarely remembers her mother but thinks often of her father, whom she obviously loved very much and whom she lost when she was about sixteen or seventeen. The novel also insists that Anna is not, at first, particularly attracted to Walter. She recognizes that he is rich, admires his clothes and his style. She is also curious about sex. But when, after their first dinner in a private dining room with an adjoining bedroom, he kisses her, she senses that he is assaying her in much the same fashion that he earlier sniffed the cork of the wine they would consume, and she "hated him" for so obviously reducing her to a connoisseur's dessert. She resists his sexual advances. The evening proves to be a fiasco, which is perhaps why he subsequently sends her a brief tender letter and five five-pound notes. He wants to demonstrate that he is not the poor dolt that he seemed to be. Perhaps, too, he suspects that his unsolicited gift might be his best solicitation.[9] If so, the ploy works. Taken suddenly ill, she writes to him: "Would you come and see me, please? . . . I mean if you care to. My landlady won't want to let you up, but she'll have to if you tell her you're a relation and please do come." He comes; he sees how sick she is; he goes out for supplies and even buys an eiderdown in response to Anna's complaints of being "so cold." She requires the fatherly ministrations at once provided by this man old enough to be her father. In short, lost herself and lost mostly because of her lost father, Anna is particularly vulnerable to the ambiguous attentions of a prospective lover who at first promises to be a stand-in for the missing parent.

Because Anna readily "succumbs" to Walter's

"wiles" it is easy to blame her for her own suffering and setbacks. As conventional wisdom dictates, she should have known better. Peter Wolf, for example, wonders what the girl expected when she let herself be picked up in the street, and observes that "a friendship that starts in the gutter usually stays there."[10] But such accounting for the character's plight overlooks the author's accounting of how she got there in the first place.

Rhys tellingly depicts how lowly situations breed unlikely hopes and how those unlikely hopes are the precise handles whereby the low can be further exploited. Thus the dance-hall girl, wishing to escape from the dull circle of her demeaning life, is ready–even calculatingly ready–to fall in love with and marry some well-to-do man who solicits her attention. But her calculation is neither so crude nor so accurate as his. She dreams of an escape from her shoddy present. He knows the price at which she can be had. It is a small price, the mere semblance of a romantic interest. Furthermore, since he is, at first, definitely interested, he even spares himself the minor indignity of consciously playing the hypocrite and taking unfair advantage of the poor girl. He too, for a time, sincerely hopes that everything will work out. His "everything," however, is not quite the same as hers, and his disappointment, when the romance collapses (as it generally does), is rather easier to bear than hers. He can solace himself with another round of the same game. As damaged merchandise–increasingly damaged–she is less and less likely to land yet another man whose victory lies in not being landed.

In the demimonde world of Rhys's fiction sexual pairings constitute a kind of round dance, the gents circling one way and the ladies another. The nature of that dance is made especially clear in a central scene that turns on an oddly inverted pairing of two different sets. Walter and Anna have taken a country holiday, the first night of which is the high point of Anna's young life: "I woke up very early and couldn't think for a bit where I was. A cool smell, that wasn't the dead smell of London, came in through the window. Then I remembered that I hadn't got to get up and go away, and that the next night I'd be there still and he'd be there. I was very happy, happier than I'd ever been."[11] The next night, however, her happiness is somewhat tempered when she and Walter are joined by another couple, Vincent Jeffries, Walter's cousin, and his current mistress, Germaine. Vincent is considerably younger than Walter; Germaine is not nearly so young as Anna; the second couple, arguing publicly and exchanging glares and insults, are not so congenial as the first. Walter presently explains to Anna the reason for the others' "awful fight." Germaine is "old," admittedly not "any older than Vincent," but "that is old for a woman." Germaine "thought she had her claws well into him," yet Vincent is leaving her, and he is also leaving without providing her with "all the money she asked for." The precise sum is never specified nor need it be. For Walter, any amount would be unreasonable, since Vincent has already "given her far more than he can afford–far more than anybody else would have given her."

Despite their apparent differences, the two sets of lovers dance to the same measure. Vincent is going away. But so is Walter: "Yes I'm going to New York next week and I'm taking him [Vincent] with me." This is the first that Anna hears of her lover's impending departure; that night is the last night the two spend together. Walter departs and Anna is left desolate. So Vincent, in his acrimonious dealings with Germaine, is a cruder version of Walter, while Anna, despite her love for Walter (and she has come to love him), is a younger and much more naive Germaine. She had to have the whole interaction between Vincent and Germaine explained to her. She does not believe that Walter has really abandoned her until, at least a month later and after he is back in London again, she receives a letter explicitly informing her that he "is still very fond of [her] but he doesn't love [her] . . . any more." The severing has been accomplished with no public scenes or embarrassing recriminations and entirely on Walter's terms, which include the chief proviso that those terms never be questioned. Vincent can well aim at acquiring the art with which Walter plays his polished part, while Anna can hardly look forward to becoming even more obviously another Germaine.

An artful dodger, Walter capably sidesteps any personal or moral claims that might interfere with the life he obviously wishes to lead. Yet it could be pointed out that he does acknowledge financial claims. But his acknowledging of only financial claims and his handling of those claims constitute, I would argue, his most capable dodging. The fact that he is willing to pay for his pleasures entitles him, he would have it, to enjoy them with a clear conscience, whereupon he pays duplicitously, and just what transaction takes place when any cash is transferred remains deliberately fuzzy. "See what a generous and concerned man I am," the money seems to say as it leaves his pocketbook. Arriving in her purse, however, it delivers a different message; "Look, lady, I've already reimbursed you for the services that you rendered." Somehow she becomes a prostitute without him ever being a John. And here too business is done on Walter's terms, for it is he who decides what her price will be. He includes twenty pounds in the letter he sends her telling her that all is over, and he could have just as easily put in two or two hundred. What he will provide is up to him, as he fully indicates even with a promise of other future payments. "He wants," the letter reads, "to arrange that you should be provided for and not have to worry about money (for a time at any rate.)" That dangling parenthetical contradiction—she can worry about how long she does not have to worry—is simply one more sign of Walter's consummate hypocrisy.

A further sign is the fact that the letter was not even written by Walter. It is Vincent who provides the fatuous reassurances that run through the missive and supplement the promise of still more future payments: "You've got everything in front of you, lots of happiness. Think of that. Love is not everything"; and, "Life is chock-full of other things, my dear girl, friends and just good times and being jolly together and so on and games and books." Just as Walter earlier assisted Vincent by taking him away from Germaine, Vincent here "does Walter's dirty-work."[12] Anna, hopelessly naive as she is, needed Walter to tell her of what was happening with Vincent and Germaine. Now the end of her own affair has to be explained to her too. Walter, however, is spared the necessity of spelling out to her—and thus to himself also—the fact that she is being paid off.

Walter is portrayed as a man so adept at attending to his own interests that he simply has no glimmerings of the duplicity with which he does so. That wise innocence is his salvation, in contrast to Anna's different innocence which does not at all keep her from her fall. Thanks to these two different innocences, Walter can remain—in his own eyes, in the eyes of his society, and in the eyes of a recent critic too—"a decent man by the standards of his time."[13] Rhys, in fact, insists on his decency. He attempts to help Anna professionally during the course of the affair. Providing her with acting lessons will presumably enable her to support herself better after his departure than she could before he arrived on the scene. He is generous after he first leaves her, when it would have been quite acceptable behavior if he had given her nothing. Called upon later, he at once agrees to underwrite her abortion.[14] Yet Rhys also expects the reader to see beyond

Walter's decency, to see him outside the social context in which he can be defined as "decent," and thereby to see that context in a darker, truer light. Indeed, one of the most calculated ironies in the novel is the author's portrait of this good man as both seen and not seen through Anna's eyes.

Anna, as an inexperienced outsider encountering England for the first time, often fails to draw the right conclusion or to voice the appropriate question or comment. The reader must therefore do so for her. Thus we see, as Anna does not, how she has been defrauded by Hester, how she will be cast off by Walter. "Your predecessor," he casually observed, early in the affair, was not like you: "She was certainly born knowing her way about. It doesn't matter though. Don't worry. Do believe me, you haven't got to worry." As already noted, Walter's "not to worry" is usually freighted with the opposite meaning. Anna's predecessor predicts her successor. Anybody but Anna would see that she was simply the latest in a long line of mistresses and therefore also know what his reassurance was worth. It is the very fact that she doesn't know that makes Walter's treatment of her both more callous (he knows that she "doesn't know her way about") and more obvious.

In effect, Rhys uses her protagonist's naiveté as a lever to move the reader to unlikely judgments—judgments that do not simply reiterate the dictates of the society. One critic has even analyzed at length an example of such levering and found it "a climax of the novel."[15] Todd Bender focuses on Anna's reaction to the news that both Walter and Vincent are about to depart for an extended stay in America. During the subsequent course of the conversation between the two couples the matter of how Anna and Walter met arises. Vincent comments, "You dirty dog, Walter. What in God's name were you doing on the pier at Southsea?" When the two men laugh but

will not explain the joke to Anna who demanded to know
what was so amusing, she "jammed" her cigarette down
on Walter's hand, and they "stopped laughing." Her
reaction, Bender argues, "is as mad and destructive as
Antoinette's blinding Rochester by fire. It is self-destruc-
tive as well; because, from that episode on, Walter is set
on deserting her." Nevertheless, this critic continues,
Anna's violence "seems crazy or antisocial only if we do
not question the assumptions of the society, if we assume
that the laughter of Walter, Vincent, and Germaine is
acceptable aggression," whereas Anna's response is not.
"The thrust of the story, however, is to question that
normative framework. It is not so crazy [under the cir-
cumstances] to burn Walter's hand."[16] Indeed, considering the circumstances, we might well wish she had got the
other one too.

More minor episodes can be just as telling as Anna's
unlikely revenge (for the most part, she is a passive victim). When, for example, Walter observes that Victor has
been generous to Germaine and has already given "far
more than he can afford," Anna replies, "Oh, has he
given her far more than he can afford?" Walter's figurative dismissal of the whole matter becomes Anna's question of fact. Since Vincent appears to be considerably less
wealthy than Walter and to go through mistresses at an
even more expeditious rate, it is highly unlikely that Vincent gives any of his women very much. But the fact is
that not much is required—an occasional dinner maybe,
the pleasure of his company. And thus the larger fact that
everything is presumably in order so long as a few mini-
mal social and financial proprieties are maintained.

Anna, as already noted, reads Vincent no more per-
spicaciously than she reads Walter. Rhys's larger point,
however, is that the judgment that Anna, in all her naiveté, does not make is not the same judgment that society,
in all of its experience, does not make either. The best that

Anna can do is to perceive such superficial matters as the physical similarity between the two men. Vincent "was a bit like Walter only younger. And better-looking." Germaine can go one step further to report something of what these two similar looking men look like: "Did you see that face?" she asks of ·Walter registering his pursed-lip disapproval of the scene that she is making in the restaurant. "Well that's the way you look sometimes, Vincent. Scorn and loathing of the female–a very common expression in this country. Imitation gold-fish, very difficult." The reader must see them both still more clearly, as types of one another whose similarity best reflects the way in which their society is geared to produce men of their sort.

And women too; consider again Hester whose "motherly" concern extends only to saying just enough to the girl so that she can later claim she warned her stepdaughter and her conscience is clear. This is no less hypocritical than Walter expostulating to Anna that only virginity "matters" just before he relieves her of it. Or we might note Ethel Matthews, the older woman who kindly rented Anna a room after the breakup with Walter and who proved to be no better as a substitute maternal figure than Walter was as a paternal one. "Let me tell you that when I asked Anna to come and live with me I did not know what sort of a girl she was and she is a very deceiving girl," Ethel writes to another woman who has taken the now pregnant Anna in after Ethel turned her out. "I know what life is and I do not want to be hard on anybody," she goes on. "So when she first started having Mr. Redman to see her I did not say anything about it [she did, however, raise the rent]. He was a very nice man and he knew how to behave. But after he left she really overstepped all bounds but not in any way that you could respect because there are ways and ways of doing everything." Anna's offense was not what she did but the open manner in which she did it. She should have been a more deceiving girl or at least kept up a proper pretense of trying to deceive. The way in which Ethel herself pathetically practices the virtues she preaches, regularly asserting the respectability of her masseuse trade (probably prostitution) only emphasizes the social insistence on hypocrisy. One must keep up appearances even when there is nothing else to keep up, especially when there is nothing else to keep up.

England, for the Rhys heroine, is a land where, as an anonymous man claims early in the novel, "a girl's clothes cost more than the girl inside them." As this gentleman observes in passing: "You can get a very nice girl for five pounds, a very nice girl indeed; you can even get a very nice girl for nothing if you know how to go about it. But you can't get a very nice costume for her for five pounds." With such pricing, values are twisted and skewed, as Anna only a few times dimly perceives. There is, for example, her assessment of herself as a newly fallen woman. Back in her own quarters late one night, she reflects that "I am bad, not good any longer, bad. That has no meaning, absolutely none. Just words. But something about the darkness of the streets has a meaning." The meaning of the dark street will later become even more clear but not the meaning of her "badness." Or we might note her evaluation of purity. During the course of the meeting with her stepmother she notices an advertisement, "What is Purity? For Thirty-five years the Answer has been Bourne's Cocoa," and her mind wanders: "Thirty-five years. . . . Fancy being thirty-five years old. What is Purity? For Thirty-five Thousand Years the Answer has been. . ." (ellipsis in the original). She does not have to finish. Virginity is as much a commodity as cocoa.

Such passages are rare however. As earlier observed, Rhys mostly judges England (the country, its inhabitants, their customs and manners) through the very judgments that Anna does not make but which are worked into the structure and vision of the novel. In this respect, one major structural feature of the book is the continual juxtaposition of snatches of West Indies memories against the recording of Anna's present reality. Again and again the latter is portrayed as cold (Anna's predominate sensation throughout the novel), dark, drab, dead; the former as warm, light, bright, alive. For Rhys, the paucity of the one world is illuminated by the abundance of the other. The perversions of the one world are suggested by its intrusions into the other, as noted in Anna's scattered reflections on such matters as the extermination of the Caribs or slavery as practiced by the colonial settlers or the illegitimate half-breed children of white fathers (illegitimate according to what law?). Finally, the harsh rhythms of European life especially grate when contrasted to the more natural ways of a different life. Thus Anna remembers how her menarche was greeted by Francine, a black servant: "When I was unwell for the first time it was she who explained to me, so that it seemed quite all right and I thought it was all in a day's work like eating or drinking." But then Hester must offer her stepmotherly counsel. She "jawed away at me, her eyes wandering all over the place. I kept saying, 'No, rather not. . . . Yes, I see. . . . Oh yes, of course. . .' But I began to feel awfully miserable, as if everything were shutting up around me and I couldn't breath. I wanted to die." That concluding suggestion of entrapment, of impending interment is another hint as to the real nature of Anna's fall. The fall was into European womanhood, with emphasis on the European. For Jean Rhys, as much as for Joseph Conrad, the heart of darkness lies back in the mother country, and it is into that darkness that Anna voyages.

4

Quartet: The Fiction of a Ménage à Trois

Quartet has been "dismissed as sentimentally autobiographical, melodramatic, aesthetically unconvincing."[1] Of those three charges, the first is paramount and brings in the other two. Thus Elgin Mellown sees Marya Zelli, the protagonist of Jean Rhys's first novel, as "so much" an "autobiographical projection . . . that she fails as a fictional creation," while Harriet Blodgett suggests that "Rhys lets her own bitterness warp the presentation of Marya's trials throughout."[2] Such criticism is not surprising considering the genesis of the novel. Rhys, late in her life, admitted "that she started *Quartet* because she was very angry with Ford and wanted to pay him back."[3] Such a beginning is not auspicious. A work that tells in only slightly disguised terms of the imprisonment of the author's husband, of her disastrous affair with Ford Madox Ford who took her in when she was penniless in Paris but then dropped her, and of the subsequent breakup of her marriage is no doubt too close to too large a tragedy in the writer's life to allow her the total dispassion and control that we expect in a major work of modernist fiction. Moreover, *Quartet* is Rhys's first novel, and apprentice labors are seldom polished masterpieces. The book does evince occasional "acts of authorial clumsiness."[4] Nevertheless, as Thomas Staley argues, *Quartet*, despite its flaws, has "much to commend it as a product of the modernist movement—its sparse style, the author's gift for understatement and irony, the careful rendering of the heroine's preoccupations in a hostile, alienating urban environment."[5] This first novel is thematically significant too. Frank Baldanza observes that *Quartet* "presents the absolute confrontation between the outcast and the respectable."[6] That contrast is crucial in all of Rhys's fiction.

Quartet merits attention as Rhys's first novel. It is also her most autobiographical novel, so much so that one critic writes of "Marya *née* Jean."[7] As such, the book serves as a useful test of the hypothesis, most fully argued by Mellown, that the admittedly autobiographical early novels can be ordered according to "their internal chronology" and read as a "sequential story."[8] In this sequence *Voyage in the Dark* comes, of course, first, and then "the story resumes in *Quartet*" with the protagonist somewhat older and now named Marya Hughes instead of Anna Morgan.[9] But the reader coming to *Quartet* after *Voyage in the Dark* should see that Marya, although she is older than Anna, is not simply Anna grown older. Marya's disastrous discovery that she can depend on neither husband nor lover for love, support, or even a show of sympathetic concern is a recognition that Anna, at the end of *Voyage in the Dark*, is way beyond. In short, the two books can better be seen as parallel stories of persistent hope, the early foreshadowings of disappointment, and the full realization of that disappointment in a world that, for these heroines, makes defeat almost inevitable. *Voyage in the Dark*, written later, is not a prelude to *Quartet*, and neither is *Quartet* a sequel to the subsequent novel even though Marya, as much as Anna, voyages in a personal and social metaphoric darkness.

Quartet is particularly interesting for one other and quite different reason. It is a fictional record of what must be one of the most fruitful affairs–literally speaking–ever, for all four of the participants have written about it. To counter Rhys's *Quartet*, Jean Lenglet wrote *Barred*, his telling of what happened (or, perhaps more accurately, his retrospective version of the way he wished it might have been).[10] Somewhat more interesting is the account of the deceived "wife," Stella Bowen, who in her 1941 autobiography, *Drawn from Life*, briefly describes how the affair sundered her previously happy relationship with Ford. Bowen is generous to "poor Ford" and his propensity for messy entanglements; she can recognize her own anomalous status in the ménage, "cast for the role of the fortunate wife [she and Ford were not legally married] who held all the cards" as opposed to the "poor, brave and desperate" girl "doomed to be let down by the bourgeoisie," and can also assess the appeal of her rival, a "very pretty" young woman possessed of "a needle-quick intelligence and a good sort of emotional honesty."[11] It is not quite the same group portrait that we see in *Quartet*. But still more intriguing is Ford Madox Ford's *The Good Soldier*, an account of the affair written some ten years before the fact. This book, Ford's acknowledged masterpiece and a major twentieth-century modernist novel, is centred on Edward Ashburnham-an officer and a gentleman-who is charitably drawn towards helping damsels in distress and then drawn to something more than charity. The novel, as Paul Delany points out, "offers an imaginative justification for Ford's Good Samaritan complex" (a complex which prompted him to "help" Rhys) and also explores "his general fascination with multiple sexual relations." Thus, Delaney suggests, "Ford's household arrangements in 1925 . . . can be understood as an attempt to make his life imitate his art."[12]

Just as *The Good Soldier* can be seen as a kind of prelude to the actual affair, so too can it be seen as a prelude to *Quartet*, which constitutes, as Judith Gardiner has recently maintained, "Jean Rhys's great tribute to her literary mentor Ford Madox Ford."[13] The relationship between the two authors is complicated. He recognized her "singular instinct for form," and encouraged her to develop that talent.[14] She was his mistress and he abandoned her. She, not he, profits from that loss, the profit being the impetus towards fiction that the ending of the affair provided. She writes a novel in which he is pilloried as a ludicrous dilletante, yet that novel, in its impressionistic rendering of experience and careful control of form, pays tribute to him as a teacher. Gardiner traces out numerous parallels between the works to show how Rhys's novel proclaims "both its esthetic tutelage and its moral independence" to become "a sadder and in some ways wiser 'saddest story'" and "more truly 'a tale of passion' than the technically perfect *The Good Soldier*" on which *Quartet* was largely modeled.[15] The best revenge was, if not writing better, at least writing differently.

As Gardiner implies, the essence of Rhys's revenge is to give Ford a starring role in an inverted version of his own best novel and thereby portray him as a prig. That different view of the protagonist also questions the vision of the earlier novel. In *The Good Soldier* two of Edward's loves die and one goes insane, yet the focus is on Edward. The reader, the author, and especially the obtuse narrator are all preoccupied with the protagonist's story, with the way in which he is to be seen and pitied as the uncomprehending victim of changing mores. Rhys simply takes a female character destined to play a minor part in such a masculine drama (as, indeed, was Rhys herself) and gives the woman the starring role. With that change, we have a protagonist who is the comprehending victim of unchanging mores—a rather more representative and distinctly less common tragic figure.

The tragedy that will befall Marya is typically foreshadowed from the very beginning of the novel. Heidler is early described as stolidly immovable; a man who "looked as if nothing could break him down." Still more ominously, Marya, on first meeting him, sees in his eyes "a curious underlying expression of obtuseness—even of brutality." In contrast, Stephan is slight, unreassuringly insubstantial. He is "thin" before his arrest, "thin and furtive" afterwards. Clearly, he will be no match for Heidler, nor will Marya. But one early passage especially foreshadows some of the most crucial issues in the novel. Marya remembers her family's reservations about her decision to enter into a stage career and she also remembers how she answered their objections: "When she had pointed out that, without expensive preliminaries, she would be earning her own living, everybody had stopped protesting and had agreed that this was a good argument. . . . For Marya's relatives, though respectable people, presentable people (one might even go so far as to say quite good people), were poverty-stricken and poverty is the cause of many compromises."

Marya, too, will find poverty the cause of various compromises. The novel itself is structured around Marya's two main compromises and shows how the two cancel each other out to leave her even poorer at the end than she was in the beginning. Those two compromises are, of course, the two men in her life, Stephan Zelli and. H. J. Heidler. And that they are compromises partly mitigates Marya's responsibility for the consequences of having depended on either man in the first place. Thus Thomas Staley, for example, argues that "since she has lost one protector temporarily, and needs another, she allows herself to drift or be taken in [by the Heidlers] without weighing the possible consequences."[16] But a more pertinent consideration should be her possible alternatives, and the novel shows that there are none short of seeking employment as a *nue femme* (a nude dancer) in some low-level nightspot. The Heidlers' preferred charity could hardly be more demeaning than that.

Marya's first compromise, her marriage to Stephan,

derived as much as the second from countering considerations. She sensed, from the start, that Stephan "was
probably a bad lot," and yet, continues the same passage,
"she felt strangely peaceful when she was with him, as if
life were not such an extraordinary muddle after all, as if
he were telling her: 'Now then, look here, I know all
about you . . . I know you aren't happy. I can make you
happy." At the time she was not happy. The chorus had
proved a dead end: "A vague procession of men [all]
exactly alike." Marya, who, at nineteen, had longed to
play a "glittering part," felt, five years later, only the
"dread" of "growing old" and sensed that her options,
narrow to begin with, were becoming even more limited.
Stephan was different from all those men whom the girls
in the chorus "knew so well–'Swine, deary, swine,'"–and
that difference constitutes his charm. He "was secretive
and a liar, but he was a very gentle and expert lover. . . .
And besides, she liked him." She marries him to come
"for the first time in her life . . . very near to being
happy." Her misgivings also at first seem groundless. The
marriage works in its odd lurching fashion and despite
such setbacks as regular bouts of poverty or clear evidence of Stephan's shady transactions (at one point he
sells Napoleon's sword) about which he continues to lie.
When, some four years after their marriage, Stephan is
arrested, Marya can insist: "We've been friends. We've
had fun together. I don't care what he is."

But part of the belated price of the first compromise
is the second. The connection between the two men in
Marya's life is further drawn by the subtle irony whereby
Rhys has Stephan assume substantial responsibility for
his own cuckolding. To begin with, the timing of his
arrest emphasizes the two charges that can be leveled
against him, his dishonesty and his improvidence. The
arrest, as Stephan expostulates to his wife when she first
visits him in jail, came at "the worst" possible time,

"when I have no money." So he also finds that poverty requires compromises, and when Marya tells him of the Heidlers' invitation that she live with them, an offer that "filled her with . . . extraordinary dismay," he demands that she accept. The vehemence of that insistence—answering her reservations with, "Do you want to drive me mad? I wonder if you know what it is like for me shut up here, thinking of you without a sou"—rather rules out one critic's suggestion that Marya with "clever manipulation . . . forced Stephan" to give her "implicit moral justification" for what she already intended to do.[17] It is not Marya who here manipulates but Stephan, for he would have it at least seem that he is still taking care of his wife. Yet his exasperated charge, "Do you want to drive me mad?" shows where his main concerns lie, and where he assumes hers should also lie.

The irony of Stephan's sending his wife to live with the man who will be his successor in her bed is further compounded by the consideration that, in his dealings with Marya, Heidler is simply Stephan writ large.[18] Marya first admired Stephan for being "so sure of himself, so definite, with such a clean-cut mind." Living with the Heidlers, she immediately falls into the routine of serving H. J. his morning coffee, "for he was very majestic and paternal in a dressing-gown, and it seemed natural that she should wait on him." Here is a man more commanding in his pose of male supremacy than ever Stephan was. Even more than Stephan, Heidler also makes explicit the predominant importance of his desires and his entitlement to what he wants. When Marya objects to his first protestations of love as "rude and unkind and unfair," he "calmly" counters, "Don't be silly. . . . You've every right to be like that, and I've every right to take advantage of it if I want to. That's truth, and all the rest is sob stuff." Just as Stephan expected Marya to abide by his wishes (that is why she is with the Heidlers), so too does Heidler.

Thus Heidler's various charges that Marya is "not playing the game." The game is his game. It should be played his way. Anything else, in his own words, "will make things difficult for me . . . make things so difficult for me."

To play, however, makes things difficult for Marya. To keep up appearances–part of Heidler's games as much as Stephan's–she must go along with the pretense that all is well with the Heidlers. When she can no longer bear the covert indignities that Lois, in retaliation, piles on her or accept her position in the house as something between a mistress, a rival, a junior wife, and a charity case, she leaves to be installed by Heidler in a cheap hotel. There she is more clearly defined: "the little woman who lived in the Hôtel du Bosphore for the express purpose of being made love to, *a petite femme*." It is Heidler's definition and it serves him well. "Are you all right for money? I'd better leave some money hadn't I?" he would regularly question shortly after love-making and just before leaving with some "Look here, I must go now. Because Lois. . ." (ellipsis in the original). Forced to ask for everything he gives her, she casts herself as a kept woman, which makes him (like Walter Jeffries in *Voyage in the Dark*) a man who has paid for his pleasure. "The endless repetition" of these scenes "became a torture" to Marya but she cannot even complain of that fact: "He had everything on his side–right down to the expression on the waiter's face when he brought up her breakfast."

The full price of playing the game becomes more obvious after her husband is released from prison. Heidler then deserts her because she won't desert Stephan. "I've never shared a woman in my life . . . and I'm not going to start now," he informs Marya, and will not even contemplate the truth of her countercharge that "you forced me to share you . . . for months. Openly and ridiculously." Stephan, moreover, shares "Heidler's sexual morality" and sees the affair "solely as an insult to him."[19] Neither man will brook the possibility of a rival, so both abandon Marya. Furthermore, permanently leaving Paris for a new start elsewhere, Stephan is willing to take with him a woman of the streets whom he has just met, which, as Peter Wolfe has also pointed out, is a favor he refused his wife when she begged him for just such an escape from Paris and before he knew of her infidelity.[20]

Desperation and the dictates of her husband prompt Marya to take refuge with the Heidlers. But why does she remain when Heidler's game begins to go badly for her, as she knew from the start that it would? Rhys does not specifically pose this question and neither does she offer any comprehensive explanation for the behavior of the character modeled on herself. That restraint can be seen as a flaw in the book, a failure to work out either the psychology of the protagonist or the logic of her actions. Nevertheless, too little commentary on the whys and wherefores of the heroine's conduct serve the book better than would too much. If Marya's actions are somewhat indefensible—betraying her imprisoned husband, betraying Lois (and it was Lois, not H. J., who first took her in), betraying herself—then do not explicitly defend them, but encourage the reader to do so.

That strategy is, I would suggest, the one Rhys employs. It is a shrewd move, so shrewd that we have to look close to catch her at it. Note, for example, how Stella, Ford's common-law companion, becomes Lois, "obviously of the species wife" and, as such, "formidable, very formidable." Or Rhys, actually older than Stella, becomes Marya, who is somewhat younger than Lois. When reading the novel it is, in fact, easy to overlook Marya's age. We are, in one passage, specifically informed that she is twenty-eight, but she regularly acts more like some seventeen-year-old child bride lost and abandoned in a world that she does not understand. As such, she elicits sympathy, from the readers and from the other characters in the book. Thus her "frail, childish, and extraordinarily shabby" mien when, after Stephan's arrest, she first visited the Heidlers.

Rhys also provides more substantial evidence out of which the reader attuned to the nuances of the text can build a case for Marya. There is first the weighty consideration of economics, of poverty and its attendant compromises. Stephan, penniless and arrested, is better off than Marya, penniless and free. He need not worry about his room and board. She has to stoop to the indignity of being taken in, and then that compromise is itself further compromised when Heidler exploits her poverty through the calculated investment of his generosity. Some months pass before he admits that he "is tortured by desire" and "wanted [her] the first time [he] saw [her]." Marya is quite right in pointing out that there is something "abominably . . . unfair" in that declaration. If he wanted her from the first, he should have told her from the first. She would have known that it was not any kindness on his part that prompted his charity and could have clearly refused or accepted the full terms of the offer—his room and his person. What he has done is to conceal the second term in a deceptive package deal. She accumulates, under the false pretenses that the assistance provided is all free, a large debt of gratitude, whereupon he presents the bill. Can she then, after all that he has done for her, simply walk out on him?

Marya's material poverty is itself compounded by what we might call her social and psychological poverty. Her marriage to Stephan severed her from her family and her chorus-girl friends, limited as those connections were. For four years her social world had been only Stephan. His arrest severs her from him too, and not just because he will be for a year in jail. The physical separation becomes a psychological one, as Stephan withdraws into "the circle of his own pain" to become "unreachable"

(Marya's term) right at the time when Marya most needs him. She cannot talk with him about going to the Heidlers, even less can she talk about the crisis that arises after she has gone, which further complicates that crisis. Heidler's declaration of love, twisted as it is, is still a promise of a human connection extended to a woman who has been for some time quite alone. Rhys also astutely suggests the power-politics psychology that underlies the beginning of the affair. Because Marya is substantially helpless herself, she exaggerates and idealizes the power she sees in Heidler, who does have power over her in that her very survival seems to depend on remaining in his good graces. She also aspires to play a larger role in his life, to be more than an object of charity and thereby assert the importance and validity of her own life. That traditional trap works in the traditional way, which is to say that Heidler himself is no more or less honest than others of his kind. His offer of love is a promise of service: "'But I want to make you happy,' he exclaimed loudly. 'It's my justification that I want to. And that I will, d'you hear? In spite of you, I'll do it!'" The service of love is a further subjugation—"the rules of the game." It is a difficult game for those demeaned by its contradictory rules. No wonder Marya plays it badly.

The course of skewed love never does run smoothly. But Heidler, refusing to notice the obvious impediments in his way, lurches over them rather more roughly than necessary, and it is Marya who takes the lumps. The most obvious of those impediments is Lois. One of the few touches of comedy in the novel is Heidler's repeated claim to complete matrimonial independence as contrasted to his diffident philandering. "Lois and I go our own way and that's been the arrangement for some time," he argues with Marya, "Lois simply doesn't come into this at all." He wants to make his position clear at the time because "Lois will come in, in a minute," and when

Marya observes that Lois is in, "I heard her some time ago," Heidler bustles out from the younger woman's room. If adultery requires, as Hester Prynne in Hawthorne's *The Scarlet Letter* maintained, "a consecration of its own," these comic scenes emphasize how little Heidler is committed to Marya and consequently how empty their affair is.

The wife is a problem for the mistress in other ways too. It is she who practically pushes Marya into the affair and who will not hear of Marya's departure once it has begun. Lois officially ascribes to the philosophy of always giving her husband what he wants. "D'you suppose that I care what you are, or think or feel? I'm talking about the man, the male, the important person, the only person who matters." Unofficially, however, she wants the affair close at hand where she can keep track of what is happening, help it to go badly, and be on the scene to pick up the pieces (and considerable credit for her tolerant forebearance) once it has collapsed. Indeed, Marya's bitterest pill is that she must finally deal with Heidler only through Lois. The husband gives his mistress's last pathetic letters to his wife to take care of, and Lois thereby triumphs over her rival. As Marya at one point notes, both Heidlers were "inscrutable people, invulnerable people, and she simply hadn't a chance against them, naive sinner that she was."

Just how little a chance she has is made clear at the end of the novel when the trio of the whole middle section becomes a quartet again. Stephan is released from jail. He and Marya now differently counterpoint the central duet of the Heidlers who even at the height of the affair could still strike the same note, "both so often [observing to Marya] in exactly the same tone of puzzled bewilderment; 'I don't see what you're making such a fuss about.'" It is, to say the least, a disharmonious counterpointing. Stephan has been allowed only a few days' grace before he must leave France. During that time, the Heidlers invite the Zellis to dinner. Both men try to claim Marya; she resists Heidler's attempt to appropriate her in the presence of her husband; he is humiliated; Lois can finally, as she planned all along, console her "poor, poor H.J." for being caught in a situation so "abominably [Lois's term now] sordid." After that pathetic party, the final partings begin. Stephan cannot afford to take Marya with him when he leaves, as required, for Amsterdam. Heidler—to prove that the affair is over, to pretend that it is not, and to reassert some sense of his own control—sends Marya for a vacation to the south of France with only enough money to pay her hotel expenses. Desperately unhappy, she writes, pleading in the name of love, that he allow her to come back to Paris and see him a few more times. He has Lois convey his regrets, which, for Marya, is "like being stripped and laughed at" by the triumphant wife.

The love that does not move Heidler does not move Stephan either. Just as Heidler was early portrayed as a Stephan writ large, Stephan is finally seen as a Heidler writ small. The husband, not prospering in Amsterdam, returns illegally to Paris in preparation for a still more radical new start elsewhere. He sends Marya the money that allows her also to return to Paris, at which point she knows that she cannot put off any longer the confession that she has several times earlier tried to make. She also hopes that he might be able to help her in her "terribly unhappy" state and appeals to him, in the name of love, to do so. He admits the terms of her appeal but only until he hears that she was Heidler's mistress and Heidler has (in Stephan's term) "chucked" her. She is, he then insists, a "fool" who has "only [herself] to blame." He voices grandiloquent threats of immediate revenge, which prove to Marya that he, as much as Heidler, "didn't care a bit what happened to [her]." She now sees him as "the symbol of

everything that all her life had baffled and tortured her"–
baffled and tortured her, it might be added, by refusing to
see her. She will retaliate; she will be noticed: thus the
claim of still loving Heidler and her threat of reporting
Stephan to the police. The claim was "only [intended to]
hurt him," the threat was immediately rescinded;
nevertheless, he struck her "with all his force" and leaves
her "crumpled" and "still" with no more than "*Voila pour
toi*"–so much for you. So much for the love he so recently
asserted.[21]

The last scenes have been criticized as contrived and
melodramatic.[22] Yet they do complete the drama of
Marya's sacrifice on the altar of love and also make clear
the final inversions that leave her desolate. To start with,
Marya, with her confession, plays to Stephan in much the
same fashion that he has just previously played to her. She
prefaces her admission of infidelity with, "I can't any-
more–I can't. I must be comforted. I can't any-
more. . . ." Those words should recall the way he, only a
few pages earlier, began his admission of failure in
Amsterdam–an admission that definitely touches her: "I
can't any more. You don't know what it is. I can't. I've
cried myself to sleep like a little boy night after
night. . . ." The point of this similarity in pathetic
acknowledgments of defeat is, of course, the difference
between the responses elicited. She did "know"; she
could respond sympathetically; at Stephan's words, "her
heart twisted with pity." Her confession, however,
merits no sympathy but a blow which well might have
killed her.

At the end of the novel Stephan does not play Marya
to Marya's Stephan. Instead, he plays Heidler, right-
eously indignant that a woman could expect him to love
her still. "I have a horror of you. When I think of you I
feel sick," Heidler had proclaimed. Stephan says so too,
but with violent action, not with words. Both men can be

disgusted by a woman who has done exactly what it suited them, when they were in slightly different circumstances, for her to do. It should also be noted that Stephan does not play Lois to Marya's Heidler. The conclusion of the novel casts the four characters into two overlapping triangles; Lois and H. J. are married and Marya is the intrusive lover; Marya and Stephan are married and H. J. is the intrusive lover. When both triangles collapse, we see Lois welcome Heidler back and even attend herself to some of the messy little problems of ending his affair. Stephan, however, acts in no comparable fashion. The rules of the game are clearly different for betrayed wives as opposed to betrayed husbands, for straying men as distinct from straying women.

When he leaves the dead or unconscious Marya, Stephan departs to play Heidler in yet another sense. On the stairwell he meets the current girlfriend of his current protector, a man Stephan met in prison and who has provided him with the money he needed to come back to Paris as well as a place to stay while he is in hiding there. He is "going off," Stephan mentions to the woman. "Take me with you," she suggests in her "very pretty voice," and he does. That last action perfectly demonstrates the hypocrisy of Stephan's outrage at that which had been done to him. Heidler, he claimed, deserved to die for messing with the woman of another man. Yet here is Stephan making off with the woman of his one friend and patron. Marya was totally beyond the ken for being unfaithful. She deserves no consideration at all for the circumstances that might have driven her to betray him. Yet here is Stephan taking up with a woman who changes her men as readily as she might change her underwear. It is a grimly comic note on which Rhys ends but it somehow does subsume together all that is, for the author and her protagonist, rotten in the state of romance, and rotten, finally, because of the biased and hypocritical "rules of the game."

5

The Art and Economics of Destitution in *After Leaving Mr. Mackenzie*

Quartet is the story of a woman arriving at the nadir of her existence; *After Leaving Mr. Mackenzie* is the story of a woman residing there.[1] Julia Martin, the protagonist of the latter novel, is, in a number of respects, a Marya Zelli grown somewhat older and more beaten down. Both have been abandoned in marriage; both are abandoned out of marriage too. Each is an almost masochistic character who occasions the suffering she endures and each is also—a paradox central to all of Rhys's fiction—an innocent victim of circumstances (and men) that she cannot control nor even comprehend. Despite the similarities between the two protagonists, they are not, however, essentially the same character at different levels of a descending life, and there is no need to consider *After Leaving Mr. Mackenzie* as simply one more voice added to *Quartet's* song of sorrow. Marya is devastated by her tragedies, whereas Julia finds in hers some means of enduring them. The one is left for dead at the end of *Quartet* (and perhaps is dead); the other, at the conclusion of *After Leaving Mr. Mackenzie*, more accurately measures the emptiness of her life and survives through what well might be termed the power of positive desolation.[2] One feature of Rhys's fiction is that her novels, all similar to one another, are also all surprisingly different from one another.

Like Rhys's other novels, *After Leaving Mr. Mackenzie* is the story of a woman more left than leaving. The novel begins in Paris in the springtime, but in that hallowed romantic setting, the protagonist, a "*jeune dame*" of thirty-six, enjoys no April rejuvenation. Julia's fall, Rhys demonstrates through an inobtrusive chronology carefully worked into the novel, continues into spring and beyond. Left early in October by Mr. Mackenzie, her latest lover, Julia has lived for six months on the weekly allowance that he has continued to provide. Her first crisis is a substantially larger check (one thousand five hundred francs instead of the usual three hundred) and the promise that there will be no more. Julia seeks out Mackenzie in his favorite restaurant, slaps him, and flings his money back at him. While doing so, she is observed by Mr. Horsefield, an Englishman vacationing in Paris, who soon becomes Mackenzie's successor and who almost immediately provides Julia with the same sum that she has just thrown away. That money returned enables her to journey to London to see her family (a dying mother, a jealous sister, a selfish uncle), to seek financial help from the wealthy older man who was her first lover (he had promised that they would always be friends), and to continue her affair with Mr. Horsefield. All three objectives come to nothing. Ten days after her voyage to England Julia returns to Paris; ten days after her return to Paris she once more encounters Mr. Mackenzie who buys her a drink, sadly observes how "suddenly" she has gone "phut," and obliges her when she requests a "loan" of one hundred francs. On that declining note the novel ends.

The argument of the plot thus summarized is not promising, and yet Rhys everywhere gives her story unexpected depth and complexity. We might note, for example, how *After Leaving Mr. Mackenzie* opens with a half-reversal of the usual fate of the usual demimondaine protagonist. Instead of ending with this foreordained victim seduced and abandoned, we commence that way. Or more accurately, we half-commence that way. Julia Martin was not exactly seduced in that she readily acceded to Mackenzie's original advances. She is not exactly abandoned in that six months after he decided to take himself out of her life he is still paying her three hundred francs a week, which is enough for her to go on living modestly in Paris. But not exactly living either. For the six months following Mackenzie's departure, Julia has immured herself in a room in a cheap hotel seeking mostly "a good sort of place to hide in . . . until the sore and cringing feeling, which was the legacy of Mr. Mackenzie, had departed." Her refuge is also the setting for a sustained but hopeless rage. Often she would "walk up and down the room consumed with hatred of the world and everybody in it. . . . Often she would talk to herself as she walked." As Thomas Staley has observed, references to ghosts run throughout the novel.[3] The first ghost is Julia herself haunting her quarters and her own empty existence.

There is a definite point to the protraction of that haunting, which is to say that Rhys has her reasons for beginning the book with the aftermath of a crucial parting and not with the preliminary relationship or even the parting itself. In the first place, the separation is standard, predictable, part of the normal course of affairs. Why note what has often happened before? What has not happened before is Julia's sense of being "done for" after being put down yet another time. The reader might therefore wonder at first what was so special about Mr. Mackenzie (we never learn his first name) that his loss mattered so much. The answer, the novel soon shows, is nothing; Mackenzie is no different from his numerous predecessors; he treats Julia no differently from the way they all have done. But that "no difference" finally makes a difference, and Julia breaks after being dropped once more in just the same fashion as she has been dropped numerous times before. The retreat from life, the emotional debilitation, the futile rage that Julia sees as "the legacy of Mr. Mackenzie" is also the legacy of all who have preceded him. One unlikely reaction sums up the previous course of a too common life.

Rhys also uses her protagonist's initial contradictory reaction—such a minor cause, such a major effect—to suggest something of the contradictions inherent in that protagonist's previous life. Julia, we are one time told, had gone from "artist's model" to "mannequin" to "principally living on the money given to her by various men." That third mode of supporting herself on the basis of her good looks occasions a delicate question as to this character's actual profession just before the beginning of the novel. Is she a woman selling herself to a limited clientele and for no set price or is she a woman too ready to fall in love with some man from whom she can then accept assistance because financial gifts are tokens of his love for her? In simpler terms, is she essentially a mercenary or essentially a romantic? The answer, of course, is that she must be both—and neither. Physical survival demands the former and precludes the latter. Psychic survival demands the latter and precludes the former. These fine considerations would not apply, of course, if the woman were simply a prostitute for whom cash received for no services rendered would pose no problem. But Julia's problem, at the beginning of the novel, is that she must insist her dealings with Mackenzie were not primarily commercial despite the fact that she has long been taking his money. Such sustained pretense, incidentally, is also required for the greater satisfaction of her customers. The men in Julia's life are as determined as she to define their dealings with her as affairs of the heart, not affairs of the pocketbook.

We might also note that Julia originally thought that "a week or perhaps a fortnight" would suffice as a post-

letdown recovery period. Six months later she is no
nearer a cure. That contradictory conjunction of an
optimistic prognosis and a prolonged devastation reflects
Julia's basic strategy of surviving crises through the odd
ploy of both denying and indulging them. Indeed, Rhys
suggests her protagonist's capabilities as a victim-endurer
even with the first sentences in the novel: "After she had
parted from Mr. Mackenzie, Julia Martin went to live in a
cheap hotel on the Quai des Grands Augustins. It looked
a lowdown sort of place and the staircase smelt of the
landlady's cats, but the rooms were cleaner than you
would have expected." The cheapness of the hotel is
countered by the grand address; the rooms, cleaner than
you would have expected, are not necessarily as clean as
you might have wished, and the stairway smells of cat. So
is the hotel acceptable, bearable, or not? The question is
hard to answer, and that surely is the point. What I am
arguing is that Rhys, in portraying her protagonist and
her protagonist's situation, strikes from the very start a
strained balance correlative to the way Julia balances herself on the edge of her professional dependency. We have
the facts of Julia's physical and psychological destitution
and countering those facts we have the ploys whereby
Julia attempts to retain some semblance of self-respect.
Note, in this context, the very first words of the novel and
how the deliberately indefinite formulation, "After she
had parted from. . . ," serves to suggest, as does the title
itself, that Julia has left Mr. Mackenzie without exactly
denying that he has thrown her out.

   Julia's careful balancing allows her to live on the
limited resources available to her. Yet that same balancing, we soon see, sometimes costs more than this character can afford. There is, therefore, a double irony to the
author's double-entry bookkeeping of her character's
psychological and social losses and gains. Even the first
entries, the claims Julia makes for herself—the hotel is not

so bad, she has not yet become the "hideous" old woman upstairs—attest by their very paltriness to her desperate plight. But that plight becomes even more desperate when yet another transaction must be doubly entered. Julia received Mackenzie's unexpectedly large last check. That same night she seeks him out and makes a scene. Flinging the money into his face is "one of the most stupid, self-defeating acts she could have done."[4] But it is equally a desperate gesture of independence. She does not need his money, she must insist, precisely because it is all she will receive and she needs it more than ever.

There are still other contradictions in this charged encounter. The scene with Mackenzie will punish him for abandoning her, first as his lover and then as his officially abandoned lover. But punishing him, she also, with clear Freudian implications, punishes herself, first for allowing herself to be bought when she entered into the relationship and second for allowing herself to be paid off when he exited from it. With such behavior as returning Mackenzie's money or returning herself to London and to the family and former lover who all want her elsewhere, Julia enforces a subconscious sentence against herself. In short, Rhys shows that even as her protagonist acts to deny a crisis ("I am an honorable woman and I won't take your [Mackenzie's] money"), she also acts to make it worse ("I am a destitute woman and must accept whatever money you [Horsefield] will give me and on whatever terms you give it"). In the duplicity of that double action Julia also both penalizes herself for how low she has fallen and demonstrates the justice of her punishment.

Consciously, of course, Julia would vociferously deny the verdict that she, in effect, passes on herself. She is, she would have it, mostly the victim of circumstances—circumstances being mostly a shortage of cash. "You see," she had one time argued with Mackenzie, "a time comes in your life when, if you have any money, you can go one way. But if you have nothing at all—absolutely nothing at all—and nowhere to get anything, then you go another." She thereby asserts that she is not responsible for the expedients she has been forced to embrace. Yet that rationalization, Rhys shows, takes Julia further down the road she would have supposedly preferred not to take and serves substantially to make her into the woman whom she claims only circumstances forced her to become.

Rhys early incorporates into the novel a calculated reference to a still larger dichotomy implicit in her protagonist's story. When Julia encounters Mackenzie at the restaurant she gives vent to her hitherto repressed anger: "It was like a flood which has been long dammed up suddenly pouring forth." Yet he is not at all moved by the torrent of her grief and rage: "He listened, half-smiling. Surely even she must see that she was trying to make a tragedy out of a situation that was fundamentally comical. The discarded mistress. . . . A situation consecrated as comical by ten thousand farces and a thousand comedies." He would make a farce of her tragedy, and furthermore the whole weight of cultural tradition supports him, not her. After all, how can all those comedies be wrong? Rhys's task, of course, is to show that they are wrong, that we have all been conditioned to evaluate romances gone astray in ways favorable to the men thereby discomfitted. The author would have us read Julia's story to correct the conventional misreading of that story. The protagonist's suffering demands attention, not the "Mackenzieish" dismissal of "well, what did she expect if she chose to live that way?"

Rhys gives substance to a story of suffering by giving it form. What might otherwise be merely the ongoing saga of Julia's setbacks—a kind of soggy reveling in protracted sorrows—is subtly cast into a three-part tale that circles back, appropriately, to its own approximate origins. That three-part progression is, it should also be noted, underlined by the geographic unfolding of the plot. The first four chapters constitute part 1 and, beginning with Julia abandoned in Paris by Mr. Mackenzie, tell of her crucial encounter with him, her subsequent meeting with Mr. Horsefield who gives her the same amount of money that she insisted on returning to Mackenzie, and of her decision (made possible by the recouping of that loss) to return to London. Part 2, the bulk of the novel, chronicles in fourteen chapters her misadventures in London. We see her disappointed by her family, by her elderly first lover (she has believed his long-ago parting admonition that if she should ever need. . .), and finally by Horsefield himself. In part 3, only three chapters long and hence the briefest section of the book, she is back in Paris again and in retreat in another cheap hotel very much like the one in which she was originally in hiding.

The concluding three chapters do not, however, quite balance the opening four. Julia's world, small as it was, has contracted still more, and her options are even more limited than they originally were. To return again to London, for example, is, at the end, quite out of her reach. The form traced out during the course of the novel is not, then, a circle–a line of narrative bent round to return to its own origin as does, say, James Joyce's *Finnegans Wake*. Instead, Rhys's narration bends back to its beginning but falls short of it, which gives us, to translate the novel into spatial terms, a geometric figure that corresponds to one full turn of a spiral. The ending of the circled novel is totally open; the action portrayed in the plot can be imaginatively extended in endless repetition. The spiraled novel is both open and closed. The plot imaginatively extended can be represented as a single line of action often repeated but still circling towards its own vanishing point.[5] The resultant figure of a vortex descending to nothingness is also clearly suggested in the novel itself. At one point Julia stands looking long "at a picture representing a male figure encircled by what appeared to be a huge mauve corkscrew. At the end of the picture was written, '*La vie est un spiral, flottant dans l'espace, que les hommes grimpent et redescendent très, très, très sérieusement*'" (Life is a spiral suspended in space, which men ascend and redescend very, very, very seriously).

Form substantiates the story, and details substantiate the form. For example, Rhys provides a number of seemingly minor facts to conjoin the first part with the third one while also differentiating them one from the other. Thus the gift of one thousand five hundred francs that brought Mr. Horsefield into Julia's life is not exactly matched by the later gift of ten pounds that apparently takes him out of her life. Or Mr. Mackenzie's final large sum which she returns to him in the first section is partly returned to her as his small "loan" of one hundred francs in the third section. And to consider all of her men and their money, we can note that Julia boasts to Mr. Horsefield, in part 1, about her London friend, "a very rich man," and how readily "he'd help me." The friend is Mr. James; the help is all of twenty pounds, which serves only to take Julia back to Paris and part 3.

Two noteworthy chapters, "The First Unknown" in part 1 and "The Second Unknown" in part 3, provide another example of Rhys's unequal balancing to achieve connective contrasts between the novel's beginning and its end. In each case Julia is approached by a man who intends a pickup in the streets. She denounces the first stranger for his presumptuous insult of, in effect, labeling her a prostitute. He denies the charge: "Not at all. . . . I have some money and I am willing to give it to you. Why do you say that I am *ignoble*?" For him, obviously, ignobility and insult lie in proposing to enjoy the favors of an unknown lady without at least offering to pay. Yet Julia is still buoyed up by this encounter, and back in her room "her forebodings about the future were changed into a feeling of exultation." She can think, as "she looked at herself in the glass . . . 'After all, I'm not finished. It's all nonsense that I am. I'm not finished at all.'" It is the second stranger who finishes her when he sees her more clearly during the course of the second pass: "'*Oh, la la.*' he said. '*Ah, non, alors,*' [and] he turned about and walked away." His look of "deadly and impartial criticism" strikes her like "a blow over the heart." The blow is her recognition of her value in his eyes, even though she had no intention of bargaining with this prospective buyer either. Nevertheless, a nontransaction still leaves her both sold out and worthless at the end of the novel. The further irony is that it is unknown men, not the known men in her life, who most determine what her value must be.

As earlier noted, Rhys does not validate what would be the conventional reading of her protagonist's story. But neither does she validate her protagonist's own reading. Just as the unequal balance between the first part and the third gives us the form of the novel, the two chapters, "The First Unknown" and "The Second Unknown," are the fulcrum upon which that balance turns. It is through these two unknowns that we best know Julia, for it is her failures to read these readings (and the men who provide them—as unknown to her as she is to them) that show her reading of herself. Essentially, she is, throughout most of the novel, a blank page upon which others can inscribe whatever value they wish, and that then *is* her value. So the two episodes in which Julia is differently priced by two nameless men appropriately frame most of the action in the novel even as they also emphasize what we might term the protagonist's "commodityness" and provide a paradigm for her dealings with all other characters. Rhys's point is clear. Having no money of her own, Julia is worth just what some man (even a total stranger) will pay to have or not to have—it does not matter which—her company. Valuing herself in this fashion, as she does until the very end of the novel, Julia seems no more disposed to take control of her own life or even to determine the direction of her fall than is a leaf in the wind.

Yet Rhys also shows that the obvious fecklessness of Julia's life is not the whole story, and that this character's resolute refusal to admit to motives does not prove that she hasn't any. "I don't know why I came. A sort of impulse, I suppose," is how Julia at one point "explains" her return to London. Admittedly, her decision to make the journey was consciously determined on less than rational grounds:

> She thought: 'If a taxi hoots before I count three, I'll go to London. If not, I won't.'
> She counted, 'One . . . Two. . .' slowly. A car shrieked a loud blast. (ellipsis in the original)

Yet we still note the fudging here—the slow count, the fact that a "car" is not necessarily a "taxi"—and note also how fortuitously chance pushes Julia in the direction she will not admit she wishes to travel. She had already decided that she "must go away," that some escape from the mess she has made of things in Paris was "the only thing to be done." The money recently acquired from Horsefield makes that escape possible. Even better, it means that she can go home in some semblance of style, not as an obviously abject and defeated woman. Still more important, Julia wants to meet again with both her mother and her first lover as a kind of symbolic coming to terms with her own beginnings as both a woman and a certain kind of woman. And that large purpose serves a still larger one. A disastrous present prompts a return to the past that might provide the basis for a different future. In short, Julia is making a desperate attempt at some kind of rebirth.

It does not work; the journey to London comes to nothing; the return to Paris marks the three-part structure of the book and establishes the pattern of Julia's life. Implicit in that pattern is one of Rhys's subtlest ironies, for it is the protagonist's covert effort to alter the course of her existence that most attests to the downward spiral characteristic of her previous life. That life had been, of course, a round of men. Each man had represented a possible new beginning, a chance that this time it might be different, although it never was. In short, things after leaving Mr. Mackenzie continue to be much as they were before meeting him, and the specific setbacks Julia suffers in her attempt to escape, even briefly and geographically, the failure she has made of her life are themselves, as a brief analysis can show, versions of that failure.

To consider her first London failure, from the very beginning Julia's efforts to reestablish a relationship with her family are muddled. In need of validation, she also needs the badges of an assumed success. And again Rhys shows how her protagonist's desperate remedies only compound the problems they were intended to cover over. Because Julia, before coming home, has spent most of her money on clothes, she must plead poverty to Norah when they first meet in the cheap, dingy hotel room that Julia can barely afford. Resentful of her sister who has not sacrificed herself for their dying mother ("And who's better dressed–you or I?"), Norah refuses Julia's implicit and explicit requests.[6] She will not lend her any money; she will not even allow her sister to stay a few days in the family flat. Norah already has "a friend . . . a trained nurse" living with her to help with the mother, "and there's not a scrap more room in the place." Julia thus becomes an occasional bystander to her mother's dying; her limited role is directed not just by Norah but also by Norah's mannish friend, Miss Wyatt; the end result is a bitter quarrel with Norah immediately after the mother's death. That quarrel ends with one of the protagonist's saddest setbacks, Julia "being put out of her mother's house by a stranger."[7] And here is one of Rhys's grimmer "home truths": Home, when you have to go there, is not always the place where they have to take you in.

Julia is dispossessed even during those times she can spend with her dying mother. The daughter never consciously acknowledges to herself what she wants (a ploy that obviously serves to blunt her disappointment when, as she suspects will be the case, her want is thwarted), but it is clear that she hopes for some sign of concern, acceptance, love. When the unconscious mother is beyond making such a sign, the most the daughter can do is to recollect a past that does not provide a base for some brave new beginning in her unhappy present. Julia's earliest memories of how as "a very young child she had loved her mother" who had then been "the warm centre of the world" are inextricably mixed with memories of how she had been pushed at age six from the center of this world by the birth of her baby sister. Another female took her place in a crucial pairing (the story of Julia's life); that first pairing inverted still persists, with Norah now babying their dying mother in a manner that leaves no place for Julia. Witness, for example, the end of the first meeting with the mother: "Sometimes anybody strange seems to upset her. Go on; you'd better go," Norah orders, and "Julia went out of the room listening to Norah's crooning and authoritative voice. 'Don't cry, my darling. Don't cry, my sweet. Now, what is it? What is it you want?'"

Paralleling Julia's return to her young childhood past is her return to her young womanhood past, which is also an attempt to come to terms with another crucial abandonment. After the long afternoon spent with her unconscious mother, Julia pays an evening call on W. Neil

James, the man with whom she had, at age nineteen, her first affair. Here too, Rhys hints, her protagonist has certain covert expectations. Again, Julia wants a sign. And this time she receives it, but the sign received is not exactly the sign she wanted. Indeed, the scene between these two former lovers covertly at cross-purposes shows us Rhys at her tragicomic best. Mr. James treats Julia as an old friend even though he is thinking how "tactless" are such "resurrections of the past." Julia is uneasy in Mr. James's presence, as if he were an "important person" to whom she was appealing and not an old friend. His polite request as to how she is doing elicits the honest answer that such a question is not intended to provoke. She would briefly describe the downward tenor of her life after she and he parted, in the hope that such a confession might be a possible preliminary to some form of absolution. He does not want to hear, for the saga of her setbacks can hardly gratify his vanity, considering his role in the tale. She wishes for some evidence of real concern but, with her characteristic inability to articulate to others or herself just what she wants, can only hint of money.[8] Or perhaps the confusion lies elsewhere. After all, money is, in Julia's world, the best proof of concern. In any event, he is angered by her not so covert plea—but also relieved. The promise of money can shut her up, and he promises. So she does receive a sign that he cares, and what he mostly cares for, in the present as in the past, is to preserve his own equanimity. The sense of self-complacency that his twenty pounds purchases is cheap at the price. That twenty pounds defines her too—in the present as in the past. The gift received is, as were, undoubtedly, "gifts" before it, a payment for services rendered—not for sex this time but for a kind of masturbatory stroking of his ego. Just as it was with the mother, so is it with the lover. Julia's attempt to find in a problematic past a retreat from an impossible present gives her a parodic version of both her present and her past that is more demeaning than either was in its original form.

A spiral, however, spins both ways, and if the picture of the corkscrewed man sets forth a transsexualized synecdoche of the novel, it should also be remembered that the sentence appended to that painting observed that men clamber up as well as slide down life as a spiral. In different terms and in keeping with the double-entry "bookkeeping" whereby Julia conducts her life and Rhys portrays it, we can observe that just as Julia's small triumphs often come at large cost, so too can her major setbacks bring her unexpected dividends. In this context, let us look again at Julia's London failures, starting with her inability to establish any connection with her family and with the breach between the two sisters.

When the two women first meet after a ten-year separation each reads in the other the story of the intervening years. Norah notes that Julia "doesn't even look like a lady now." But Norah too "was labelled for all to see." "Trained to certain opinions which forbid her even the relief of rebellion against her lot," Norah is exactly what Julia is not, the quintessential "good girl" who will act exactly as she is supposed to act. The novel dramatizes the differences between the two women and it also dramatizes how little difference that difference makes. If Norah, then, represents, for Julia, the accepted and expected road, the road Julia has not taken, what Julia and the reader both see during the course of the older sister's attempt to ground herself again in her family and her past is Julia's justification for having struck out on her own. Admittedly, she ended up lost, but, as she later also admits, she at least "had a shot at the life I wanted." Norah has had the invalid mother for six years and a life she sums up as "like death . . . like being buried alive." And it is Norah who is, in a sense, the less honest of the two in that "she wants the very thing that she despises her sister for enjoying."[9]

The contretemps with Norah serves to dispel any possible sad regrets regarding a misspent life by forcing Julia to contemplate in Norah the proper woman whom Julia herself might have been. The reencounter with Neil James provides another corrective disillusionment. As we have seen, Julia had considerably romanticized her first affair. But Rhys also shows how Julia is brought to revise her earlier self-gratifying revision as to the facts of the case. Shortly after the final meeting with Mr. James, Julia observes to Mr. Horsefield that she really knows little about the other man–then or now. "You see, he never used to talk to me much. I was for sleeping with–not for talking to." It is not a flattering assessment, but she does at last know where she stands, and where she stood.

It is this knowledge that partly redeems the conclusion of *After Leaving Mr. Mackenzie*. When Julia, back in Paris, asks Mackenzie for a "loan," there is a continuing element of self-deception in the terminology that she employs. Nevertheless, she then knows what she is after. She wants the money as money, not as a sign of something else (his continuing concern, say). Although Julia is finally reduced to obvious mendicancy, asking solely for the cash, she is also more successful than when she earlier asked for something more. Presumably she will continue with that greater success in a game more demeaning (she is now a beggar) and less (she is no longer, in effect, hypocritally prostituting herself), which is another reason why the ending of the novel is not irredeemably bleak.[10] Julia sits alone with the second drink Mr. Mackenzie bought her: "The street was cool and full of grey shadows. Lights were beginning to come out in the cafés. It was the hour between the dog and wolf, as they say." This poetically suggestive final sentence moves, as does the symbolic spiral, in two directions. Darkness is descending, but Julia, with a drink and some cash, is partly provided for, and there are some lights to counter the coming night. The hour of the wolf has not yet arrived (the reference here is not to men as sexual "wolves"–that time has come and gone–but perhaps to the finally untamable aspects of life, to the mother howling and dying as an animal); meanwhile Julia has become somewhat more adept at managing the dogs in her life.

There is one final turn to the ending that Rhys appropriately appends to this subtly plotted work. The symbolic spiral in the painting is "*flottant dans l'espace*." "Floating in space," it is supported by nothing, rested on nothing. And as Helen Nebeker especially observes, nothing is, indeed, a key issue in the novel.[11] Julia's earliest memories are of being happy because of nothing and then of being frightened by nothing. At one point in part 1 she describes one of her failures to give an account of herself: "And I felt as if all my life and all myself were floating away from me like smoke and there was nothing to lay hold of–nothing." By the end of the novel, she better knows the nothing that pervades her life. More specifically, she knows that her role in her family is nothing; that her dreams of her first love were nothing; that her hopes for her next affair have already come to nothing. But if Julia does not quite become, with that awareness, a forerunner of Camus's Sisyphus who can happily roll the rock of her own nothingness up the mountain of the nothingness of existence, neither is she crushed between the weight of those two voids. In that strained survival we see again how completely Rhys envisions the bleak life of her protagonist right down to the small sustaining victory achieved through the way in which Julia finally confronts the unredeemed darkness of her fate and we also see how carefully the author structures the novel to sum up the emptiness of both the defeats and the victory. It is a book that is "terrible" in its vision but "superb" in its full realization of that dark vision.[12]

6

Affirmation from Despair in
Good Morning, Midnight

Good Morning, Midnight is a strikingly fitting title for a work written as Europe drifted towards tragedy, for a novel that would constitute the author's last published words for almost thirty years. It is as if Rhys was (to borrow a phrase from Robert Frost), well "acquainted with the night" on both the private and the public level and, having greeted the coming darkness, could slip into silence even as the world sank into war. But leaving writing (at least for a time), she did not depart on any declining note. This last early work is one of her darkest, grimmest, and starkest fictions; it is also, as indeed the title suggests, her most affirmative novel.

The novel itself centers on Sasha Jensen, the oldest of all Rhys's protagonists. A woman in her forties who knows that her descending life can only descend further but who lacks the courage or the convictions for an open and honest suicide, Sasha attempts a covert one. A small family inheritance allows her to set out to drink herself to death. Sasha is interrupted while doing so by an old friend who lends her still more money–not to speed the process of her dying but to send her from England to Paris and hopefully a new beginning. The City of Light, however, offers Sasha mostly more evidence of her past failures. So, "saved, rescued, fished-up half-drowned out of the deep

dark river," she still attempts to arrange her new life in the
narrowest possible terms of a cheap room in a nonde-
script hotel, "a place to eat in at midday, a place to eat in at
night, a place to have my drink in after dinner." Into this
arrangement a young gigolo intrudes. He is obviously
misled by Sasha's old fur coat and thinks she is a wealthy
woman willing to pay for the pleasure of his company.
She is doubly tempted by him, first planning to enjoy his
mistake and then hoping that some real human connection is possible. The complex interaction between these
two ends in a near robbery and a near rape. Sasha, in her
hotel room, is left desolate. Into the room comes a man
whom she has previously despised, an older, distinctly
odd commercial traveler also staying at the hotel. The
novel ends with Sasha's "yes" to this suitor even more
unsuitable than was the young gigolo, and that "yes" constitutes the crux and resolution of this difficult novel.

Even on the level of plot summary, Sasha's unlikely
assent is hard to paraphrase. Is she making do with the
partner at hand? Recognizing the narrow limits of her
life? Sacrificing herself in an act of supreme charity? It is
hard, too, to see just where this affirmation (or whatever
it is) comes from, for, judging by all that has gone before,
the final action in the novel should represent Sasha's most
humiliating defeat. Her listening neighbor, the *commis
voyageur* (the French term used for this traveling man
throughout the novel), overhears the gigolo depart and
decides that he shall fill the role that his rival has apparently abdicated. Sasha has just wept and prayed for the
return of the young man whom minutes before she had
asked to leave—whom she had also, she thought, paid to
leave. As usual, however, the Rhys protagonist is offered
much less than what she bargained for. Her eyes covered
against the futility of her dream, Sasha has visualized
every step of the young gigolo's return until, at the height
of the dream, "He comes in. He shuts the door after

him." Who "he" is is immediately clear, nor need she
look to know. The *commis* intrudes to find her lying,
naked, on the bed. When she does uncover her eyes she
sees him "looking down at [her] . . . his mean eyes flick-
ering." The woman who was ever undone by the harsh
judgments of others here confronts the most devastating
judgment in the novel. Not even, in the *commis*'s view, a
prostitute (there is no question as to price), she must, so
he imagines, accord to whatever use he would make of
her. But even in acceding to his silent insistence on sex,
she still transforms the act into something rather different
from the defeat just imaged in his eyes—and her own:

> He doesn't say anything. Thank God, he doesn't say
> anything. I look straight into his eyes and despise another
> poor devil of a human being for the last time. For the last
> time. . . .
>   Then I put my arms round him and pull him down on to
> the bed, saying: 'Yes—yes—yes. . . .' (ellipsis in the original)

Sasha's last words constitute an obvious reference to
James Joyce's *Ulysses*, which also ends with three yeses
and an assent to sex, with Molly Bloom's "yes I said yes I
will yes." That similarity, however, has been differently
interpreted. One critic, for example, argues that "*Good
Morning, Midnight* concludes on a note similar to Joyce's
Ulysses"; in both cases "the feminine consciousness" pur-
portedly achieves release "after a crisis," and the woman's
assent affirms "the efficacy of the possibility of union
between man and woman in which both natures are in
harmony and in love" despite an awareness of "the
hopelessness of such a union."[1] Another, however, hears
the Joycean echo as deeply ironic and postulates an
almost "Dostoevskian" pathos when "the repellent
traveling salesman . . . enters and takes" Sasha even "as
she moans Molly-Bloom yeses."[2] Or a third critic can
argue that Sasha's yes, as opposed to Molly's, merely

betokens the minor key of "a conventional love story" and shows us a previously "bickering" pair finally making "the transition from being neighbors to lovers."[3] Peter Wolfe also maintains that the protagonist's final assent entails a certain deserved retribution: "Because Sasha has spurned a handsome young man who craves her, she must embrace a scrawny old one with contempt in his heart."[4] Yet why, one could well ask, should Sasha endure yet another undesired sexual encounter, as if there have not already been enough of those in her past? A more reasonable suggestion is Elgin W. Mellown's postulation that Sasha, with her last words, "overcomes the drift toward death that obsessed the earlier manifestations of the Rhys woman [and the earlier Sasha] by finding . . . compassion."[5]

Mellown, however, does not adequately explain the nature of the drift, which, for Sasha, is surely more than an "adolescent [Sasha is hardly an adolescent] hate-fear of other human beings."[6] Neither does he explain how the redeeming compassion is finally discovered. Nor can he, for the compassion, of course, was present from the beginning. Witness Sasha's early memory of the partly bald old woman who came, with her grim daughter, into a shop where Sasha worked: "Oh, but why not buy her a wig, several decent dresses, as much champagne as she can drink, all the things she likes to eat and oughtn't to, a gigolo if she wants one? One last flare-up, and she'll be dead in six months at the outside. That's all you're waiting for, isn't it? But no, you must have the slow death, the bloodless killing that leaves no stain on your conscience." The issue is not so much the discovery of compassion but the question of how Sasha's ready compassion is shaped so that she can at last offer herself to the *commis*, and that issue is worked into the structure of the novel.

As Frank Baldanza has observed, "a train of . . . incidents" in *Good Morning, Midnight* "illustrates the hideous irony that the more desperate one is, the more cruelly people treat one; the more one needs help, the less one gets."[7] Such "hideous irony" should teach cynicism, not compassion. Indeed, on one level, the book is a devastating critique of a society callously unconcerned with the desperate. To quote again Mellown: "The respectable world views such women [Rhys's "demimonde" protagonists] as commodities to be bought."[8] To which the Rhys protagonist replies, "exactly," and registers just how respectable the respectable world is for viewing her in that fashion. Stella Bowen, not an unbiased witness, observed some forty years ago that Jean Rhys's cynicism did have "an unanswerable logic in it."[9] But a cynicism towards conventional values becomes, in Rhys's best fiction, something more, a radical devaluation of most middle-class standards and particularly the characteristic bourgeois concern for the small proprieties of life. It is the power of that devaluation which provides Rhys's protagonists with their unique perspective on themselves and their society–and which gives her fiction much of its peculiar force.

"Rhys's heroines saw the world from the inside rather than the outside. Her aim was the perfection of rendering private consciousness through style, not the achievement of an enlarged vision of the contemporary world."[10] But it might better be argued that these ostensibly different objectives represent a false dichotomy in the evaluation of Rhys's achievement. The inside view, properly perceived, becomes the outside one too. This "enlarged vision" is more persuasively presented in that it is never proclaimed or editorialized upon but must be achieved in the reader's consciousness as well as in the protagonist's, and achieved through the limited materials that the novel provides–the narrator's inconclusive account of and musing on the imperfections of her own life. It is in this respect that Sasha's story is both an idiosyncratic history of the setbacks and sufferings of one individual and a representative fable. We see Sasha assay the standard alternatives open to her–marriage, mother-hood, employment. We hear her assert her determination to be standard: "But this is my attitude to life. Please, please, monsieur et madam, mister, missus and miss, I am trying so hard to be like you. I know I don't succeed, but look how hard I try."

The reader also sees, as clearly as does the pro-tagonist, her various failures. The fiasco, described early in the novel, of Sasha's brief career as a shopgirl is rep-resentative. She does no better with marriage or mother-hood. Her baby dies. Even before the son is born, the husband, Enno, has already left. Twice, in fact. The first time with explanation–"'You don't know how to make love,' he said. . . . 'You're too passive, you're lazy, you bore me. I've had enough of this. Good-bye'"–the sec-ond and final time without. Nor can Sasha simply pas-sively exist, supported (barely supported) on her small legacy. "I want one thing and one thing only–to be left alone. No more pawings, no more pryings–*leave me alone*. . . . (They'll do that all right my dear.)" (emphasis and ellipsis in the original). The parenthetic retrospective prophecy acknowledges a second side to an impossible polarity. To be perpetually pursued and pawed is an unbearable life; to be left entirely alone is a kind of living death.

The protagonist of *Good Morning, Midnight* hardly supports, then, Elizabeth Abel's contention that, "al-though Rhys describes her heroine's progressive degener-ation, often in excruciating detail, she fails to provide an adequate explanation for this process."[11] With Sasha, explanations abound–explanations for the impasses in her life, for Sasha of course suffers no "progressive degen-eration." The problem is not so much to explain her emo-tional decline during the course of the novel but to explain her transcendent action at its conclusion. We have already seen the ample reasons why she well could be a hardened, bitter woman who, so one critic clearly misreads her character, "has aged and faded and become a mere shell of hate."[12] The novel, through two extended episodes set in the present time of the action in Paris, as opposed to Sasha's recurring memories of her past, conclusively demonstrates that she has become nothing of the sort. The two episodes, the protagonist's involvement with the two Russians and their painter friend and her subsequent involvement with the gigolo, also show how Sasha's present both continues and runs counter to much of the remembered past. Since the first of these episodes prepares the way for the second and since they both underlie the denouement of the novel, it is appropriate to examine briefly Sasha's first consumer question, should she buy a painting, before passing on to the larger one, should she buy a night with René.

The scene at the painter's studio is rather more problematic than the question that it poses for the protagonist. To begin with, there are the first wares that Sasha sees, fake Congo masks with empty close-set eyeholes that perfectly capture the expression civilized faces wear when they ask, "Why didn't you drown yourself in the Seine?" Sasha knows the "face" that the painter puts on his masks "very well; I've seen lots like it. . . . That's the way they look when they are saying: 'What's this story?' Peering at you. Who are you, anyway? Who's your father and have you got any money, and if not, why not?" Yet the known face does not always reveal the intention behind it. When the painter puts on the mask and, to Martinique music, dances before his new guest, does he then join the world inimical to Sasha or mock it with a fake likeness and reduce it to a performance for her pleasure?

Sasha herself cannot clearly read the intentions of the two men who take part in this scene, especially when they speak Russian. She has been brought by one of the Russians whom she earlier met to the painter's studio; the painter, Serge, soon finds it conveniently necessary to leave his two visitors alone for more than an hour; all that happens during his absence is a showing of the paintings. Yet the few comments in Russian made when Serge returns well might be, "Well, was she any good?" or "Will she buy a picture and is she going to pay up?" Sasha, however, has not been pushed in either direction and then she is even more confused when she begins to explain that she would like to buy one of the paintings but does not have enough cash on hand. The painter, with a "shout of laughter," interrupts to assert that he knew it all the time. He observes that he "likes her" and offers her the painting "as a present." Sasha counters that she would prefer to pay him later, whereupon Serge agrees that any price and any time will be fine. She could even send the money after she has returned to London. Or, he further suggests, with a gentle smile, she might repay him by selling one or two of his other works to her London friends. Declining these considerate terms, Sasha insists that she will reimburse him later that same night and with the full price first quoted. So we are back to the mask again. Has she been thoroughly conned or has she stepped briefly beyond the world of pose and pretense to pay freely the price that he, if freed from economic necessity, would never charge?

In either case the immediate result is the same. Sasha departs, "very happy" that Serge has just termed her his "Amis" (friend) and "exalted" with her purchase. Both reactions show how alive she is to even the possibility of kindness and concern. If she has been gulled, it is only because she lacks any shell of hate. It is also significant that she subsequently keeps faith, waiting when nobody comes at the appointed time to take her money and then worrying that the painter might not receive the full price when only the other Russian arrives late to claim the promised six hundred francs. The point here is quite obvious. She is several times given an excuse not to pay out money with which she can hardly afford to part. She is, it should be remembered, in Paris on borrowed funds which she has no clear means of repaying and funds which are already almost exhausted. The fact that, under such strained circumstances, she does not take advantage of any "justification" to save puts the gigolo's later surprising "goodness" when he does not take all of her money in a clearer perspective. He does not fully assert a rather forced gigolo's prerogative on her cash even though he could have done so, which is, to say the least, a rather less impressive exercise in existential honesty than is her own.

The painter also raises another existential question still more fundamental to the novel, the matter of existential charity. The Martinique music foreshadows Serge's story of the Martinique mulatto woman, a pathetic victim of prejudice, whom he had encountered once in London. This woman, who lived with a man who only tolerated her for her cooking, had gone out one afternoon for the first time in two years; had greeted a little girl who lived in the same house; and had promptly been told that the child hated her and wished her dead. The crushed Martiniquaise had come drunk and weeping desperately to Serge's door, asking for whiskey but seeking, perhaps, another solace too. "I knew all the time that what she wanted was that I should make love to her and that it was the only thing that would do her any good. But alas, I couldn't." Again a mask shadows forth two quite different possible faces. Is Serge's tale the most blatant kind of male sexism, an assumption that there is one sure cure for whatever ails a woman? Or is it such sexism partially transcended, a recognition that a woman not at all physically desirable—"She had been crying so much that it was impossible to tell whether she was pretty or ugly or young or old"—very much needed desiring and an admission that his inability to make love to her constituted his failure? In either event the story is equally significant, for it obviously looks forward to a more successful example of sex as existential charity, Sasha's "yes" to the *commis*.

Sasha is indulgent with the two Russians whom she allows to pick her up in the street despite their efforts (much like the men in her past) to voice, on very little acquaintance, a definitive opinion as to who and what she is: one "is willing to believe that I am happy but not that I am rich"; the other "is willing to believe that I am rich but . . . he doesn't think I am happy." She is touched by her dealings (compassion and/or commerce) with the painter. When she calls off the minor suit that the gloomily persistent Delmar, the younger of the two Russians, has pursued, she does so because he plays the game of courtship badly, regularly intimating that he cannot afford the gestures that he regularly insists on making. As Sasha notes, "this business of not being able to have what I want to drink, because he won't allow me to pay and certainly doesn't want to pay himself" is "too wearing." She still treats him, however, more considerately than his philosophy deserves. "Not one of the guilty ones," he has, he asserts, "the right to be just as happy as I can make myself," which is nothing but the philosophy of the "guilty ones" reduced to a nutshell. Sasha is not guilty of comparable self-centeredness when she lets him down gently and even worries about the little money that he has spent on her.

Her dealings with the gigolo are not quite as kind and considerate but neither are they the exercise in conscious cruelty that several critics have suggested: "she wounds him as she herself has been wounded by offering him money as a bribe to leave her alone"; or, "Sasha strings him along until he tries to make love to her, and she can insult him by offering him her money in place of herself."[13] Both charges presume a quite unlikely set of priorities on the part of gigolos. Does one insult a prostitute by offering her cash but not requiring any return services? Since the gigolo is, in effect, a prostitute who diligently pretends that he is not–all that he claims to seek, after all, is a forged passport, as if rich, lonely, older ladies have ready access to such documents–it would seem that the real insult would be to insist on the real transaction: I pay you; you satisfy me. But it is quite clear that the insult in the novel is his treatment of her, not hers of him. Sasha recognizes at once the implications of the young man's approach: "Of course. I've got it. Oh Lord, is that what I look like? Do I really look like a wealthy dame trotting round Montparnasse in the hope of–?" The dash says it all. She has hitherto been deemed sexually available by most of the men whom she has encountered, a judgment convenient for them and demeaning to her. Now she is to be worse than available; desperately so, eager to pay.

Defined even more dubiously by the gigolo than by the two Russians (she is now supposedly both rich and unhappy while he also knows what would "cure" her unhappiness), Sasha decides that she just might "get some of [her] own back." She will let him recite his piece; will savor the performance of a fellow professional who thinks he is playing to an amateur; and will then "be so devastatingly English that perhaps I should manage to hurt him a little in return for all the many times I've been hurt. . . ." (ellipsis in the original). No great harm, it should be emphasized, can befall the victim of that plot, for even the most frigidly correct, "that is not what I meant at all, that is not it at all," could hardly constitute "wound[ing] the Russian [sic] gigolo as deeply as she herself has ever been wounded."[14] Sasha, furthermore, does not carry out her first intention as originally planned. In fact, she begins to have second thoughts even as she is formulating the envisioned revenge. The plan, as quoted above, breaks off with an ellipsis when one of the lines just used in the man's preliminary spiel doubly registers in her consciousness: "'Because I think you won't betray me, because I think you won't betray me. . .' Now it won't be so easy" (ellipsis in the original).

A stranger asserts friendship and confidence in order to con another stranger, and Sasha recognizes at once that she cannot simply dismiss the other's inauthentic claim. Critiquing René's technique–"I have done this so often myself that it is amusing to watch someone else doing it"– has certain unintended implications. As Mellown has rightly observed, when the "young gigolo attaches himself to her," he represents "a cruel, reversed mimicry of her own life."[15] Sasha also soon embodies herself a different "cruel, reversed mimicry" of her previous condition. She must become the calculating patron who will weigh the other's appeal, and this function disturbs her despite the fact that the terms of René's appeal are clearly fraudulent from the start. In effect, and here we see another of Rhys's most subtle points, to punish the gigolo for his presumption, she must play the same game that men have previously played with her and the game for which the gigolo becomes, at once, a reversed reductio ad absurdum. One weighs what an inferior offers as opposed to what an inferior wants and makes as much as possible of the former while doing as little as possible about the latter.[16] The point, of course, is that Sasha cannot play the game so cavalierly as the men who provide her with her models. She knows the other side.

The prospective gigolo pitching himself at a woman with no money is a parodic reflection of the different men who would have used Sasha somewhat differently in the past. Yet, despite her lack of cash, she is not as "invulnerable" as she at first assumes. The pitch, as has already been noted, is also a parodic reflection of her own past returned in the unlikely guise of René to accost her on the darkened terrace of a bar, and Sasha is soon caught up in this different image of herself. Rhys early emphasizes the crucial significance of these various reflectings with the words whereby Sasha assesses René's unlikely tale of My Escape from the Foreign Legion: "The truth is improbable, the truth is fantastic; it's in what you think is a distorting mirror that you see the truth." And in the distorting mirror of that strained defense of an obvious "story" we see one of the central truths of the novel. The metaphor of the mask, set forth in the scene with the Russians, is here explicitly succeeded by the dominant metaphor in *Good Morning, Midnight*. As earlier discussed, Sasha's unhappy life becomes, on the largest level, the distorting mirror in which she–and we–are to read the truth of her society. On the smaller level, mirror play also governs the brief interplay of the two main characters and the final break between Sasha and René.

At first René reflects mostly backwards, imaging Sasha's past and other men in that past. He tells her of his dubious London "expectations, and Sasha sees her younger self in him."[17] She is attracted to this youthful conniver "because he is in some ways like her husband of the past, Enno."[18] But more and more Sasha begins to see, reflected in René, an image of her present quite different from the lifeless, hopeless scenario that she had previously envisioned for herself.[19] The professional and quite insincere patter of his line–and she knows it for what it is–can still prompt her to reevaluate and redefine her life. Thomas Staley has summarized this matter nicely: "René's gaiety and ebullience have lifted her out of herself. What we begin to see here as Sasha becomes witty, charming, clever, and sarcastic, is a creature who has always had these qualities but has never had the opportunity to reveal them. This transformation is one of the novel's most important elements and the narrative skill with which it is executed is a brilliant achievement."[20]

An equal achievement is the narrative skill with which the slow positive transformation is suddenly undone. That undoing, brutal as it is, is also essential to the structure of the book. The dark vision of life that informs all of Rhys's work and especially this novel could hardly be sustained by some concluding "release and liberation" through a brief exercise in role reversal brought on by a misunderstanding that was itself originally occasioned by René's misreading of Sasha's old fur coat.[21] In short, a fortuitous good morning, morning is not a recognition of abiding night, and Sasha's rosy hopes for a new dawn of love and happiness are all dashed in much the same way that those same hopes were engendered, through the truth that is implicit in the distorted pictures that René persistently throws back at her–the truth, this time, of René.

Since a prospective patroness should not finally feel that she should not have to pay, René all along modifies his flattery of Sasha. When, for example, she jestingly claims that she is "a cérébrale," he, not joking at all, responds, "I should have thought you were rather stupid." Such demeaning intensifies as their relationship moves toward its conclusion, and not only because of the practical considerations prompting the gigolo to counter a proclaimed attraction with an implied disgust. Just as Sasha is reflected in René, he also sees a reflection of himself in her. But Rhys emphasizes the crucial difference in that double imaging. Sasha would embrace the picture of herself implicit in René's flattery, while he must deny the picture of himself implicit in her manipulated response. In short, he is not, he insists–and this is part of his calculation too–a gigolo. She will accommodate him but it must *seem* as if he is accommodating her (the essence of the gigolo: "'Would you give me the money to pay for dinner now instead of in the restaurant?' he says, in the taxi. 'I'd prefer that'"). Then, in the restaurant, and even more afterwards, René, very much like the Russian, Delmar, would also prefer that her wants accord exactly to his own. The progression d'effet here is most effective. Delmar wanted the woman to want only what Delmar wanted to pay for; René wants her to want only what René also wants her to pay for. The pretense that his need is really hers is crude in the extreme: "'You're such a stupid woman,' he says, 'such a stupid woman. Why do you go on pretending? Now, look me straight in the eyes and say you don't want to.'" That directive perfectly captures the tone of one particularly disgusting attempted seduction that Sasha earlier remembered from her past—"'Can you resist it?' 'Yes, I can.' I said very coldly. . . . 'Stupid, stupid girl,' he says, doing up buttons"—and at that time she was not expected to finance the privilege of being had. In short, Sasha encounters, with René, another of the various impasses that beset her life. Of course she wants to, but not on his terms.

Her ultimate disappointment is all the greater in that it briefly seemed that they might make love on her terms after all. Finding René, as much as Delmar, "too wearing," she tells him good-bye at her hotel door. The scene that ensues is carefully set. He follows her into the hallway and turns off the light as she is fumbling for her key. They embrace, appropriately, in the dark. Sasha's hopes soar: "Now everything is in my arms on this dark landing—love, youth, spring, happiness, everything I thought I had lost. I was a fool, wasn't I? to think all that was finished for me. How could it be finished?" In the dark, she can dream of figurative dawns; in the room and in the light again, she encounters, in the fullest symbolic sense, the midnight promised by the title. The anticipated sexual encounter turns into a near rape. And here too the critics have also dealt rather dubiously with the novel's protagonist. The problem is not at all that Sasha's concern with "reputation still overrides sexuality" or that she is "too out of touch with her instincts to have sex with René."[22] Neither can we accept Staley's postulation of a "schizophrenic" split between "the passionate woman seeking but unable to accept even a fleeting moment of human passion" as opposed to an "aging, lonely female who has narrowly survived the advances of a gigolo."[23] The problem is that this split is not Sasha's but René's. In her hotel room, he again insists that the passionate woman must also be the pathetic, aging, lonely female.

> 'I knew you really wanted me to come up—yes. That was easy to see,' he says.
> I could kill him for the way he said that, and for the way he is looking at me. . . . Easy, easy, free and easy. Easy to fool, easy to torture, easy to laugh at. But not again. Oh no, not again. . . . You've been unkind too soon. Bad technique. (ellipsis in the original).

Again she refuses to accept what he offers on the terms whereby it is offered.

He insists that she is "playing a comedy," but the comic-tragic-farce of the final encounter is played mostly by René. The image of her that, so he loudly insists, characterizes her dealings with him cancels out the counter image of himself—defined by his dealings with her—that he is especially determined not to see. Thus his assertion that she is playing a ludicrous courtship game, the standard game in which the man must overcome the woman's false resistance so that they both might enjoy what the man, the realist all along, knows that they both desire. The end result of that self-serving "logic" is a twisted justification of rape, a justification so twisted that the rape is not admitted even as it is advocated: "'There's a very good truc,' he says, 'for women like you, who pretend and lie and play an idiotic comedy all the time.'"[24] Furthermore, the rape René proposes is not grounded in false logic at all but in self-deceived anger. "'Je te ferai

mal,' he says. 'It's your fault.'" What he thinks he means
is why does she pursue the courtship game of female play-
acting so badly? What he really means is why does she not
play his game of male play-acting better, play it exactly as
he would like it to be played?

Sasha counters first by mocking the play. If it is comedy he wants, she devastatingly observes, it is comedy he
has achieved: "'We're on the wrong bed,' I say. 'And with
all our clothes on, too. Just like the English people.'"[25]
She also points out that he can spare himself the "trouble"
of the rape and "have the money right away," an argument on expediency that irrefutably dismisses his and
demonstrates where his intentions have lain all along. As
he himself has maintained, why dwell on irrelevant preliminaries when one can proceed directly to the essential
matter. "'Yes, you're right,' he says. 'It would be a waste
of time.'" His game finally comes back to him as she
requires him to confront his real purpose and the image of
himself which that purpose proves. The mirror implications of this interaction are further emphasized in the text
by her last view of René in action. Before she covers her
eyes, unable to watch him take the last of her money, she
sees him looking at himself in the glass.

What he sees is implicit in what he subsequently
does. Rhys does not succumb to any false romanticism
here either. René does take some cash. Sasha had 1,350
francs; she had told him to take the thousand franc note
but to leave the small bills or she would "be in an awful
jam." He took, she soon discovers, only two of the small
bills to leave her, most surprisingly, 1,200 francs. It is a
touching gesture. "Not used" to such "courtesies," she
repeatedly toasts the "chic gigolo," the "sweet gigolo,"
and then falls into an inebriated dream-hallucination of
the world as a senseless surrealistic machine, a dream
from which she awakens envisioning the possibility of
still another chance at rebirth through the gigolo's return.

That last hope, as earlier noted, is instantly dashed by the entrance of the *commis*. Wearing his white dressing gown, he is still dehumanized in the first sense suggested by that gown—"the ghost of the landing" who had long haunted her doorway—even as he has also become some "priest" of the world just dreamed as a dead "white steel" machine.

It is at this point, in the face of what well could have been the most devastating setback of all, that Sasha transcends all her previous defeats and also refutes the death of human values—"Venus is dead; Apollo is dead; even Jesus is dead"—implicit in her dream. And again I would suggest that previous criticism has not done her justice, perhaps because it is most difficult to render in prosaic terms the subtly suggested private and poetic intimations of her triumph. "After using all her mental energy to will René to return to her, Sasha must resign herself to the reality of a *commis voyageur*."[26] Such a formulation, the depleted woman accommodating herself to the imperfections of mundane existence as embodied in the *commis*, falls short of the mark. A better reading of Sasha's final victory depends, as I earlier suggested, on a recognition of how the ending relates to all the rest of the novel.

The first crucial point is obvious. "I look straight into his eyes and despise another poor devil of a human being for the last time." The final four words of that sentence do not cancel out the first fifteen. She hates him even as she promises to renounce her hate. So, despite that promise, the present scene remains one of the most gruesome renderings (the truth in the distorting mirror) of the war between the sexes in all literature. We see the frozen moment before an act of sex that is also an act of rape (hints of René again, but now the man is totally undesired and hates the woman for the very desire that she inspires in him). She looks with loathing on him and he looks no more kindly on her. Once more two characters stand as opposed glasses, each imaging the other in the worst possible light. But now Rhys plays a most significant variation on that redoubled doubling. Sasha seizes, for the first time, another side of what we might call the judgment game—"But by God, I know what you are too, and I wouldn't change places." Briefly put, she recognizes the figure in the mirror, the commonality of all ostensible antagonists. She thereby judges her own previous judging to see that she and the *commis* are equally—the wording here is significant—"another poor devil of a human being." It is a simple enough recognition but under the circumstances it is also transcendent. Equally to the point, her immediately subsequent "yes," it should also be noted, is "yes" to a different kind of love, one that depends entirely on her. She will now define, for herself, whether what she does is love and what her love is. We see action as projection, not reaction to reflection. And consequently there is no need to worry, as Peter Wolfe does, whether or not "her heartbeat [will] strike a friendly rhythm in the *commis*."[27] For the first time, it simply does not matter.

The second and final point is that the way to this triumph is clearly pointed out to her during the course of her two previous encounters. At the end of the novel she enacts a better version of the painter's story about himself and the Martiniquaise. He could not bring himself to make love to the woman who seemed "turned to stone." The *commis* had earlier seemed, for Sasha, "a paper man, a ghost, something that doesn't exist." If love (or sex) can help, she will give this nonbeing a chance at life, the chance that Serge could not give to the mulatto woman and that René so decisively failed to provide for Sasha herself (and René's name ironically means, of course, "rebirth").

Yet in Sasha's last action René too plays a part. When he takes only a little of her money he partially redefines his role in the middle of a game that was going badly. That exercise in, essentially, modifying judgment and saving face (switching masks before the mirror) later gives Sasha her necessary cue. The distorting mirror sometimes lies, must be made to lie. René reaches that conclusion seeing himself in the mirror of Sasha, she reaches that conclusion seeing herself in the eyes of the *commis*. Each thereupon asserts through an unlikely act a different judgment, she again more convincingly than he. That different judgment brings her the only morning she will have, which comes, of course, in the middle of her darkest night. It is an ambiguous affirmation, yes to the morning and yes to the night; but it is an affirmation that rings all the louder because of the very darkness in which it is grounded.

7

From *The Left Bank* to *Sleep It Off, Lady*:
Other Visions of Disordered Life

Jean Rhys, it will be remembered, wrote short stories as well as novels. Her first book was *The Left Bank and Other Stories*. Her last creative works were two collections of short fiction, *Tigers Are Better-Looking* and *Sleep It Off, Lady*. These three volumes bracket her five novels, but they also parallel them, for both the first stories and the final ones evince, as I will subsequently demonstrate, Rhys's characteristic craft and control and are surprisingly effective in capturing, often in very short compass, the same idiosyncratic view of life that informs her longer fictions. *The Left Bank* is therefore (and despite some weaknesses in the stories—which are hardly surprising in a writer's first work) more than just a promise of better things to come, and neither are the last two volumes a reworking of old material on a smaller scale and a sign of diminishing artistic power. All of Rhys's stories can stand alone. But they stand more firmly in conjunction with the novels and, taken with the novels, they both fill out and more fully specify this author's vision of her world.

To start with the first volume, *The Left Bank* is, as its title suggests, partly grounded in Paris and on the wrong (or right—it all depends on one's point of view) side of the Seine. But the locale of these stories is not so restricted as that. As Ford Madox Ford observes in his preface to the collection, "every great city has its left bank." Furthermore, the longest tale, "Vienne," is set not just in that city but also in Budapest and Prague, while at least a few of the stories, such as "Again the Antilles," obviously takes place in the West Indies, and a few others—for example, "Hunger"—could well take place anywhere in the world. Indeed, the setting for all the stories is, in one sense, universal.[1] They portray not so much different physical places but a pervasive state of dispossession and disjunction that can sometimes be discerned in even the most outwardly regulated of individual lives. Thus the narrator of the first selection in the volume, "Illusion," is called upon to take some clothes to the hospital for a sick acquaintance and thereby discovers that plain, proper, and always soberly garbed Miss Bruce has for years bought gorgeous gowns but only to hide them in the back of her closet.

The art of "Illusion," it might also be noted, is appropriately underplayed. Neither the first mistaken vision nor the latter amended one is at all emphasized, and the narration at first seems to be little more than simple objective reporting: "Miss Bruce was quite an old inhabitant of the Quarter. For seven years she had lived there, in a little studio up five flights of stairs. She had painted portraits, exhibited occasionally at the Salon." This opening portrait of the painter as a middle-aged lady is sustained not by the fact of her profession but by a few attendant quirks—how little Miss Bruce's "British character" is touched by "the cult of beauty and the worship of physical love" going on "all round her." And at the end of the story, despite her secret being known, she is still the same person. Dining again with the narrator, she briefly dismisses the secret gowns and then notices a striking neighbor: "'Not bad hands and arms, that girl!' said Miss Bruce in her gentlemanly manner." It is hard to say whether this ending makes her more pathetic or less.

The other stories in the volume are generally simple in technique (direct first-person or third-person narration) but they vary widely in scope and effect. For example, the shortest tale in the book, the two page "In the Luxemburg Gardens," tells of a young man who quickly passes from "meditating on the faithlessness of women" to attempting another pickup, as apparently reported by the Garden itself (the Garden has witnessed many such scenes). "Trio" is also most brief, a three-page sketch describing three blacks thoroughly and quite incongruously enjoying themselves in a Paris restaurant, but it resonates with larger implications when the narrator notes, in the final sentence, how the scene observed reminds her of her own lost Antilles. "Vienne," however, at some sixty pages, is almost a novelette. The retrospective narrator of this work weaves, through what only at first might seem a series of disconnected memories, a persuasive picture of life at the edge in the Europe of the twenties—individuals straying beyond the boundaries of the law in countries approaching the verge of social collapse.

As even the titles suggest—"In a Café," "Mannequin"—a number of the selections in *The Left Bank* are almost slice-of-life sketches. Some of these are clearly sliced so as to serve up obvious indications of social injustice and brutality. "From a French Prison," for example, centers on an old man and a small boy (perhaps his grandson) who, visiting an inmate, are as hopelessly caught in the rules of the prison as is the prisoner in the prison itself. Or, in "The Sidi," we see an Arab imprisoned (perhaps unjustly) and then callously killed through violence and neglect while he is awaiting trial. Or still other stories briefly show different sides of the same suffering, as when "Hunger" (a first-person meditation on how it feels to go five days without food) is immediately followed by "Discourse of a Lady Standing a Dinner to a Down-and-out Friend" (a first-person musing on how awkward it is when an acquaintance does not manage her life better).

Other works, however, are more oblique and problematical renderings of inescapable human limitations and also of the partial transcending of those limitations. Thus the probably mad painter in "Tea with an Artist" cannot bring himself to part with any of his paintings, but he does impressive work. His wife, a former prostitute, has the soul of a peasant. He knows that she will sell or simply burn all of the paintings the moment he is dead. Yet the two of them, in their odd way, are happy, and she, with her total indifference to his art, has, paradoxically, become its best subject. And even more problematic is Dolly Dufreyne of "In the Rue de l'Arrivée." This protagonist tries to drink herself into a mental stupor as an escape from her despair at recognizing how low she has already sunk. Having sunk still lower and going home drunk, she is accosted by a fellow denizen of the lower depths whom she insults for trying to pick her up. When she receives sympathy instead of a countering insult, she begins to see, with "extraordinary clearsightedness," that only the "hopeless" and the "unhappy" can be "starkly sincere" and thus samples "some of the bitter and dangerous voluptuousness of misery." Only the fact that we are also told that she was "weeping gently but not unhappily" swings this delicate balance of small victory and utter defeat a little to the positive side.

But perhaps the most successful early tale is "Vienne." This last story in *The Left Bank*, like the first one, turns full circle but in a larger and more complicated circle. The narrator begins with the fact that, except for a "few snapshots," Vienna has all "slipped away." She goes on to remember her life there with her husband and their small circle of acquaintances, particularly noting the love affairs of one friend and the different women he took until one more capable woman thoroughly took him. She recollects her rise in the world, as her husband's financial dealings–which he would not at the time discuss with her–succeeded, and how she found him considerably more voluble in Budapest when his bubble schemes had burst and, well into his employer's money, he faced the prospect of prison; how she talked him out of the suicide he melodramatically but not too seriously contemplated; how they made their way across the frontiers of countries preparing for war or revolution; how, in Prague, they went for one last ride in their fancy car (which was already sold), while she hoped that he would understand, would crash it, and she would "scream with laughter at old hag Fate because I was going to give her the slip," but he only–the story's end–returned them to their hotel.[2]

Of course the retrospective narration has indicated from the first that "Vienne" will not end with the protagonist's demise. But it makes no triumph out of her continuing survival either. Indeed, the death she did not gain in the last paragraphs allows her precisely those other limited possessions–the "few snapshots"–that she can still claim in the story's beginning. A life redeemed only by a few photographs is still very much in question, which is to say that, in prospect and retrospect, the narrator valorizes the death that eluded her. But matters are not that simple either; the deeper irony in "Vienne" is that the story itself becomes both an extension and an analogue of those early noted photographs. Mixing memory and desire, the narrator transforms the disconnected sketches which make up her account into a series of moving pictures that are equally the record of her possession and her loss.

"La Gross Fifi" from *The Left Bank* also merits brief assessment both for its intrinsic quality (Thomas Staley finds it "the most sustained narrative in the collection"[3]) and for the way in which it anticipates other stories that Rhys will publish some fifty years later. Roseau, the narrator of the work, is a young woman at loose ends in the south of France. She is staying in a disreputable resort hotel, is in the process of being left by the latest man in her life, and is ambivalently acquainted with a few more proper vacationers whose petty hypocrisies assure her that she does not want to belong to their world but whose cutting cliquishness also attests that being excluded carries its disadvantages too.

The center of the story, however, is Francine (Fifi) Carly, and a very imposing center she is—vastly overweight, rakishly overdressed, forty-eight, and frequently attended by a strikingly handsome gigolo just half her age. Roseau has to explain to one of her English acquaintances, a young husband who has joined her for a drink in her hotel restaurant, that, no, "the gentleman" with Fifi is not her son, and then she also has to explain just what it is that he is: "Don't you know what a gigolo is? They exist in London, I assure you. She keeps him—he makes love to her. I know all about it because their room's next to mine!" But if Roseau can hear Fifi in love, Fifi can also hear Roseau in loneliness. That same night the older woman, prompted by the younger woman's weeping, comes into her room, tenderly undresses her and puts her to bed, maternally comforts and counsels her, and becomes a kind of improper friend in obvious contrast to the proper ones.

Fifi's advice is simple and to the point: "One nail drives out the other nail." Roseau is still young and beautiful. Fifi will help her to find another man perhaps more "chic" than the last one. That advice is soon given more point by the fact that it might well apply to Fifi too, who definitely is not young and beautiful. The next morning, when Fifi's gigolo returns after having been away all night, Roseau hears the two of them quarreling bitterly and then passionately making up. A week later, however, he is gone again, this time for a longer time. "Fifi in ten days grew ten years older," and not just because she has been abandoned but also because of the not-so-covert sneers and jeers that the abandonment elicits from all the proper people who never approved of Fifi and her gigolo in the first place.

The story ends with the gigolo returned again, with Fifi "radiant" at the "triumph" of the second reconciliation and agreeing to celebrate the event by an excursion to Monte Carlo, with Roseau reading in the next day's newspaper of "YET ANOTHER DRAMA OF JEALOUSY." A young man has killed his older mistress. "Questioned by the police he declared," the account states, "that he acted in self-defense as his mistress, who was of a very jealous temperament, had attacked him with a knife when told of his approaching marriage." The following morning Roseau decides that she must leave the hotel. As she is packing, she comes across a book of French poetry that Fifi had earlier given her and reads one passage that particularly appealed to Fifi: "*Maintenant je puis marcher légère, / J'ai mis toute ma vie aux mains de mon amant*," which was earlier translated in the story as "I can walk lightly for I have laid my life in the hands of my lover." Roseau then weeps "heartbroken" for "poor Fifi" until "she imagined that she saw her friend's gay and childlike soul, freed from its gross body, mocking her gently for her sentimental tears," whereupon "she dried her eyes and went on with her packing."

The story closes on that problematic note. There is something suspect, for Roseau, when she weeps, and there is something suspect, for the reader, when she stops. This contradictory and inconclusive ending is not resolved by arguing, as does Peter Wolfe, that a crucial line from the poem underlies Roseau's tears: "*J'ai mis toute ma vie aux mains de mon amant*," this critic maintains, "tells [Roseau] that she could never love as wildly or as beautifully as Fifi."[4] Taken in context, however, the line hardly validates wild love. Fifi did put her life in the hands of her lover, and the story graphically attests to what end. He threw her–her love and her life–away; first and figuratively by leaving her for another woman, second and finally by murdering her when she made a fuss about it (and of course he murdered her, for even if she had attacked him–which is highly unlikely given what we have already seen of Fifi–once he had taken the knife from her he certainly does not have to stab her to death to keep her from injuring him). A better reading is Staley's suggestion that "the power of the story resides in Roseau's implicit recognition that her life is somehow anticipated by Fifi."[5] In short, it is herself that Roseau weeps for, and it is also Roseau who knows that those tears are futile. There is a Fifi in her future; the most that she can do is be ready to meet, with something of Fifi's elan, an older, sadder version of herself. One nail drives out another in more ways than one.[6]

The youthful author of "La Gross Fifi" creates a character who reads in an older other woman something of what her own fate will probably be. Some fifty years later Jean Rhys can acknowledge just how valid that early written reading was. "Old age, she admits," paraphrased at the conclusion of Judith Thurman's 1976 profile, "is as terrible as she always knew it would be."[7] And at the conclusion of her career she can write firsthand about what she then knew firsthand. Some of the most impressive stories in both *Tigers Are Better-Looking* and *Sleep It Off, Lady* as well as the final tales in each volume (not considering the selections from *The Left Bank* reprinted in *Tigers Are Better-Looking*) are studies of old age and impending death in which Rhys graphically portrays the burgeoning ills that declining flesh is necessarily heir to.

One of the best of these late works is the penultimate tale in *Sleep It Off, Lady*, a tale which also provides that volume with its title. The protagonist of this work is Miss Verney, an elderly spinster of "certainly well over seventy" who lives alone in a small rural cottage. She is at first mostly content with that arrangement but is perturbed by a singularly ugly shed that comes with her property and that, decrepit and dilapidated as it is, still threatens to outlast her. She is even more perturbed when she discovers that a large rat has taken up residence in the shed. She observes the rat walk regally across its dominion ("*I'm the monarch of all I survey. / My right, there is none to dispute*"), and soon discovers just how valid the Gilbert and Sullivan claim that she voiced for the creature actually is. Certainly she cannot dispute the rat's rights, while everyone disputes hers. The local builder who first agrees to tear down the shed simply does not come at the promised times, which presently conveys to the old lady the clear message that he has no intention of doing the job. A representative from a larger firm in a nearby town comes once but only to assure her that he knows better than she what it is that she should do. The shed might be used as a garage by the next residents, and she doesn't want to decrease the value of her property, does she? A local man first puts out poison and then wonders aloud, when that doesn't work, if perhaps the rat weren't pink. The neighbors know that Miss Verney drinks.

The rat that occupies her shed soon occupies, in a different sense, her cottage too. Morbidly afraid of the animal, she tries not to think of it, but nevertheless it dominates her life. She almost barricades herself in her house; is careful about how she opens even a window; and "spent hours every day sweeping, dusting, arranging the cupboards and putting fresh paper into the drawers" – as if a rat on the premises well might be the immediate result of even the smallest oversight in one's housecleaning. She even dreams about the rat at night. Thus preoccupied, her life changes. She no longer goes for walks or visits with her neighbors. She eats less and drinks more. Her health suffers, which soon brings her to a doctor's attention. He prescribes pills, a telephone, and no strenuous work.

She is still buoyed up by even this small sign of concern. The next day she has, she thinks, put the rat behind her and looks forward to installing a telephone, to talking again with her acquaintances. Then, late in the day, she remembers that she has not yet taken the garbage out. But the bin is not where it should be and neither are the heavy stones used to keep the lid on (and the rat out). Struggling to get everything in its proper place, she suffers some kind of a stroke, collapses, and discovers that she cannot move even after she has recovered consciousness. Helpless on the ground, "surrounded by torn paper and eggshells," she can only call for help. Her predicament is noted only by the ominously odd daughter—a girl who never plays or smiles—of a neighbor. Asked to have her mother call for help, the girl answers: "It's no good my asking mum. She doesn't like you and she doesn't want to have anything to do with you. She hates stuck up people. Everybody knows that you shut yourself up to get drunk." The "horrible child" concludes, "Sleep it off, lady," and went "skipping away." Miss Verney can only lie in the deepening darkness waiting for the advent of "Super Rat." She is discovered unconscious the next morning and dies soon after of, the doctor concludes, shock and cold and her heart condition. "Very widespread now—a heart condition."

These last words, presumably the doctor's, ironically sum up the impetus of the whole story of this protagonist dispossessed. In the present tense of the narration Miss Verney was given no past, no abiding story to speak of, nor was she allowed even the distinguishing mark of a noticed first name. Her death too is robbed of substance and dignity and not just by its grotesque circumstances and brutal cause but also by the way it is so readily reduced to something apt, appropriate, expected,

.and dismissed. Furthermore and as Wolfe rightly emphasizes, the protagonist's demise perfectly symbolizes her society's view that the proper place for the aged is some figurative dust bin.[8] The prevalence of that view tells us, of course, just how validly the doctor spoke even as he definitely misdiagnosed who it was that suffered from that widespread heart condition.

Or we might briefly consider the three late stories in *Tigers Are Better-Looking* as studies of characters at the end of their tether. In "The Lotus," for example, an older woman living in a dank basement apartment tries to claim a small place in the lives of a young couple higher up in the building and the world. The husband is willing to patronize Lotus Heath as an amusing "old relic of the past," but his wife will not tolerate the other woman and drives her away with crude insults such as comments on her "awful" odor of "whisky" mixed with "mustiness." Later that same night Lotus goes out drunk and naked into the street. She is soon picked up by the police who return her to the building and try to find out something about her. Questioned, the young man claims to know "nothing" of the disreputable woman and neither, he asserts, does anyone else. And he is, of course, quite right, but not in the sense imagined. The story ends with the husband back in his quarters "admiring the way Christine [had] ignored the whole sordid affair" and preparing to make love to his "lovely child" of a wife. Time will inevitably acquaint these two with just what it was that troubled Lotus Heath.

The subsequent "A Solid House" takes place during the London Blitz, but the protagonist, identified only as Teresa, is much more affected by the slow collapsing of her own life than by any falling German bombs. She had earlier sought death through an overdose of (probably sleeping) pills only to dream ("But were they dreams?") of a journey through a landscape that—with a still and leaf-clogged river, an "empty and dilapidated house," a rocking horse beneath a tree, and two oddly emblematic statues of a man and woman—was as poetically evocative of death as the journey described in Emily Dickinson's "Because I Could Not Stop for Death." When her suicide fails, she takes refuge in another dwelling. Correlative to that surviving life is the structure in which it continues, "the solid house of the story's title [that] stands in a bomb-gutted city and lodges frightened, broken tenants.⁹ Presiding over this establishment is Miss Spearman, a sharp, angular, and nearly deaf old woman from whom Teresa imagines she might learn "the real secret" of "how to be exactly like everybody else" and thereby survive in the world. But Miss Spearman's "sidelines" are secondhand ladies' clothes and secondhand spiritualism. She has no serviceable secrets to impart, nor is there a place in the house for Teresa, who at the conclusion of this subtly rendered and imagistically effective tale is figuratively turning again towards the suicide that earlier eluded her.

The protagonist in the last of these three stories, "The Sound of the River," survives no better. An older couple vacationing in a cottage near a river are trying to be happy despite the continuous rain and the woman's pervasive forebodings—forebodings that prove true one morning when she discovers that the man lying beside her has died during the night. The nightmare that this protagonist awoke to on that "first fine day" continues, in a kind of Kafka sense, as she runs, seemingly without moving, to the nearest telephone to call a doctor; finds the neighbor away and the room in which he keeps his telephone locked; finally breaks into the room to reach a doctor who obviously does not believe her story when he arrives on the scene and pointedly wonders why he was summoned so tardily and did she not really know in the night that what she "thought . . . was a dream" was actually the man dying. Yet Staley still suggests that "the woman, who narrates the story, is temporarily moved out of her obsessional and premonition-laden private world by the horrible reality of the man's death."[10] His death, however, hardly makes her world less private nor proves her premonitions false, and by the same token of that death she has been consigned to a rather more threatening public world (the suspicions of the doctors) than the one she previously inhabited.[11]

Even the death described in "Sleep It Off, Lady" might seem preferable to the enduring portrayed in these three grim tales. Yet any comforting consideration that the end of life should mark the end of suffering too is countered by "I Used to Live Here Once," a two-page sketch that, coming immediately after the title story, concludes *Sleep It Off, Lady*. This appropriately final work in Rhys's fictional canon tells of a woman who, returning to what used to be her home, tries vainly to speak to two children playing in the yard. She is finally noticed but only as a sudden chill that sends the children "running across the grass to the house." And "that was the first time she knew." In eternity she has become what she was in time, a disturbing presence preferably overlooked. In short, what she is is a pathetic, yearning ghost. As A. C. Morrell, in "The World of Jean Rhys's Short Stories," rightly observes: "This bleakly poetic final vision is the most fitting culmination of Rhys's world-view."[12]

The stories in the last two collections do not, however, all focus on the old, the dying, or the dead. They do not all center on unrelieved human setbacks and suffering either. "Outside the Machine," for example, concludes with one woman patient in a hospital giving another, who is being turned out with no money and before she is ready to take care of herself, an unexpected gift of cash. If the sum is not enough to buy the recipient back "to life again," it is still "enough for a week or perhaps two" and is most welcome. Or "Let Them Call It Jazz" ends on an even more muted note of triumph. Selina Davis, a black from the West Indies who is not at all at home in London (and a narrator whose "bubbling, colorful language" is one of Rhys's "great triumph[s]" as a short story writer[13]), has finally found a small place for herself but that place has cost her her chief possession. The Holloway song (which she learned in Holloway prison) has been taken from her for a song. Some one heard her whistle it at a friend's apartment, set it down, sold it, and out of gratitude gave her five pounds. The gift at first galls: "For after all, that song was all I had. I don't belong nowhere really, and I haven't money to buy my way to belonging." But soon Selina realizes her grief is all "foolishness," for "even if they played it on trumpets . . . no walls would fall so soon. 'So let them call it jazz,' I think, and let them play it wrong. That won't make no difference to the song I heard." While the five pounds can make a small difference to her: "I buy myself a dusty pink dress with the money."

Such gains, small as they are, are rare in Rhys's fiction. The predominant direction of all the stories, including those in *The Left Bank*, is down. The characters who follow that downward course are also almost all women. As Morrell observes, Rhys's "stories insistently expose the position of the lone woman in any society, whether West Indian, French, or English."[14] That position is tenuous at best and particularly so, as Rhys shows in her late tales, for the elderly woman who has lost her youth and beauty, the capital whereby a woman is supposed to purchase a place in the world. Indeed, the plight of Rhys's older protagonists is simply the logical extension of the problems faced by their younger sisters in the other short stories and the novels. In this sense the fiction is all of a piece. "It is [Rhys's] recurrent, almost obsessive theme, that women are permanent and perpetual victims of mas-

culine society" both in its "individual" manifestations
and its "institutionalised" ones.[15] Rosalind Miles's
generalizations applies as much to the stories as the novels
and aptly emphasizes the social implications of the former
as well as the latter. So if the stories "expose the position
of the lone woman in . . . society," that isolated woman
also exposes the society.

Society is portrayed in most of the stories as stripped
down (or stripping down) to some of its barer brutalities.
Chief among these brutalities is a violence against women
that is so endemic it need not even be recognized as violence. Thus in "Rapunzel, Rapunzel," from *Sleep It Off,
Lady*, a patient in a hospital, an older woman obviously
proud of her "long, silvery white, silky hair," asks the
visiting barber to just trim the ends, but he practically
shears her and then callously comments, "You'll be glad
to be rid of the weight of it, won't you dear?" His motive
is merely to show that he can do unto her whatever he
pleases and can charge her for the injury too. Bereft of
what was most important in her life, she suffers a total
collapse, weeps continuously, and perhaps even dies (the
issue is left deliberately unclear) at the end of the story.
Or the violence can be more pointed and its motives much
more obvious, as when another hospital patient, a chorus
girl and one of the minor characters in "Outside the
Machine," briefly describes for the other patients a recent
theatrical brouhaha. A stagehand had tried to kiss one of
the dancers; she had smacked him; he had hit her back;
the dancers insisted the man be fired; they had to strike
before he was let go; and consequently, this narrator concludes, the stagehands so "hate us" that "we have to go in
twos to the lavatory." Later in the story a parson visits the
hospital and preaches to the patients on the virtues of for-
bearance and the vices of rebellion. "God is a just God,"
he insists, and "man, made in His image, is also just. On
the whole. And so, dear sisters, let us try to live useful,

righteous and God-fearing lives in that state to which it has pleased Him to call us. Amen." The stagehands' hatred and the preacher's homily expound equally the same text.

Other violences are also present in Rhys's world but are more glancingly observed. As already implicitly suggested, racial animosities underlie "Let Them Call It Jazz." Selina, suddenly evicted by her Notting Hill landlord, is no doubt another innocent casuality of the Notting Hill riots of 1958. Several of the stories set in the West Indies, such as "The Day They Burned the Books" from *Tigers Are Better-Looking* or "Pioneers, Oh, Pioneers" from *Sleep It Off, Lady*, also turn on racial tensions. Or war is seen in other tales. "A Solid House," set, as noted, in World War II, begins with Teresa and Miss Spearman waiting out a bombing raid. I would also here observe how effectively "Till September Petronella" (one of the best stories in *Tigers Are Better-Looking*) is inobtrusively dated as taking place towards the end of July and in 1914. World War I will break out in one more week. Full mobilization for that wasteful combat will begin. The various young men who were pledged to reappear, come September, in Petronella's empty life will likely find that they have other dates to keep. Mass killing can also be done quite naturally. The most graphic destruction portrayed in Rhys's fiction is in "Heat," the brief account in *Sleep It Off, Lady* of "Mont Pelée's eruption and the death of some 40,000 people."

The volcano that destroyed the Martinique city of St. Pierre is beyond control by man. Man's own violence, however, is another matter. But that latter violence is rationalized or denied by its perpetrators, not condemned or controlled. In other words, hypocrisy runs a close second to violence in all of the stories, and in some of them the contest is too close to call. For example, in "Fishy Waters" from *Sleep It Off, Lady*, the brutal assault on a very young black girl brings a disreputable white man to trial. Guilty of a smaller violence against the girl (he had threatened to saw her in half when her screams disturbed him), he is deemed guilty of the larger violence too. But after the trial the wife of the proper witness whose testimony convicted the other man begins to realize that her husband was probably the guilty party. And hypocrisy is even more central in the title story in *Tigers Are Better-Looking*, a story that itself takes its title from a brief passage early in the work: "I got a feeling that I was surrounded by a pack of timid tigers waiting to spring the moment anybody is in trouble or hasn't any money. *But tigers are better-looking aren't they?*" The tiger may eat you but it won't pretend that it is your friend first, as did Heather in this tale when she took her new acquaintances to a bar where they could be taken (and she presumably receive part of the take). The tiger has the courage of its hungry convictions and does not calculate the state of your pocketbook (as do various characters in the story as well as the police) before it springs.

The beast that springs in Jean Rhys's stories is no tiger at all but simply the world in which her characters live; the spring is typically some forced recognition of the nature of that world. So here too the short fictions supplement the longer ones to give us other versions of the Rhys heroine and other justifications for how she came to be like that. Indeed, one of the best justifications for the Rhys heroine is "Goodbye Marcus, Goodbye Rose," and I will accordingly conclude with this emblematic tale from *Sleep It Off, Lady* that effectively sets forth, both in the text and beyond it, the disconcerting validity of Rhys's vision.

The title of the story perfectly sums up the denouement of its problematic plot. Phoebe, a twelve-year-old West Indies girl, has been strangely taken up by a visiting

Captain Cardew, a "very handsome old man" and a former military "hero." He gives her boxes of chocolates, takes her on long walks, and in general treats her "as though she were a grown-up girl." In fact, on one of their excursions, he informs her that she will "soon . . . be old enough to have a lover," and immediately his "hand dived inside her blouse and clamped itself around one very small breast." Phoebe cannot cope with that action (she imagines that it is a "mistake" that he will rectify without even noticing) nor is she comfortable with his subsequent attentions that take the form of long discourses on the varieties and the violence of love. She knows that if she talked to anyone about the captain she would be both blamed and not believed. She does not know how to extricate herself without seeming babyish. She is also fascinated as well as shocked and is drawn into a complicity in this sick courtship, which soon ends with the Captain's wife condemning the girl for all that has happened and then arranging to return with her husband to England. Phoebe, left to figure out for herself what it all means, can only deduce that everything has somehow been her fault, "that he'd seen at once she was not a good girl–who would object–but a wicked one–who would listen. He must [have known]." At the end of the story she is trying to accommodate herself to this new conception of herself. So goodbye to the preteen dreams of a proper marriage and the children that she was going to have. "Goodbye Marcus. Goodbye Rose." As the children's song that she then remembers reminds her, marriage appertains only to the good. She must prepare for a different future, the prospect of being bad.

We have seen, at the conclusion of the story, how Phoebe has come to alter radically her design–admittedly a child's design–for her own life. But whether or not she abides by the revised plan is a question that cannot be answered, even though it is clear that Phoebe's conceptions of what might constitute a bad life are just as jejeune and innocent as were her immediately prior conceptions of what might constitute a good one. The story, in short, does not extend beyond the text. The criticism of it, however, does, and what is particularly revealing about that criticism is the way that it shows the tale suffering a violence at the hands of its commentators which is roughly comparable to the violence Phoebe endures at the hands of Captain Cardew. What the three critics who have written in some detail on this story all attest to, as much as does the story itself, is the social privileging, the institutionalizing, of male violence. That violence need not even be admitted as violence as long as it remains relatively discreet. Thus the captain knows that if his actions are private and stop somewhat short of actual rape, the girl is not likely to complain and will not likely be believed if she does. And Phoebe, as previously noted, knows so too. We see the latitude allowed to the captain and we see the girl blamed for his claiming it.

The man clearly abuses the trust, the body, and the soul of a child. Nevertheless, one recent critic concludes: "The lewd chatter of an old man has introduced Phoebe to the whole world of loveless sex and she accepts it buoyantly."[16] Yet what choice does she have—to accept buoyantly or to accept drowningly? And neither does her apparent willingness prove her full consent. That is the captain's logic but a logic by which, it should also be noted, he does not abide. He acts before he asks and has no intention, as the above formulation would have it, of doing her a favor. Or consider how another critic observes that "Phoebe entices Captain Cardew," that the story "recounts the events forcing Captain and Mrs. Cardew from Jamaica," but "that the Cardews stand a good chance for happiness after leaving the Caribbean."[17] This sounds almost as if the conniving young girl took advantage of the trusting old man, whose tropic vacation was

thereby cut short but who hopefully, and through no
fault of Phoebe's, will probably suffer no permanent
damage such as the collapse of his marriage. This same
critic, incidentally, elsewhere observes that "the tropics
corrode mainland codes of conduct," so that "English
people and their home-grown values come to grief in late
Rhys tales . . . [such as] 'Goodbye Marcus, Goodbye
Rose.'"[18] The poor man would have never acted that way
in England; the West Indies weather is somehow responsible. Rhys knows better what the Captain's home-
grown values really were.

Equally dubious is another's claim that even though
Captain Cardew admittedly "places his hand on
[Phoebe's] breast, he does not fondle her."[19] That simply
does not wash. This third critic, noting that "the randy
old captain . . . delights in telling her of love and passion," further evinces the same skewed perspective and
almost praises the old boy for still being so full of life.
Nor can we accept his postulation that "Phoebe is drawn
to an identification" with Captain Carew because "she
senses something wicked in him and thus in herself."[20]
Such an argument turns a powerless complicity into a willing cooperation and even, as in the first formulation, a
welcome voyage of self-discovery. It ducks the pertinent
question of what he is by dubiously discussing what she is
and making her primarily responsible for her own victimization.

For this last critic, the story reveals to Phoebe that
she has "values and sensibilities which are opposed to
those of the social world in which [she was] brought
up."[21] This is true but not in the sense implied. Phoebe
sees, in her fumbling way, how bankrupt are the social
codes that make her violation possible. To put Phoebe
somehow at fault, to attempt to valorize the ethos she is
abandoning, only proves how right she was to repudiate
it. In short and to conclude, this text especially
demonstrates that Rhys's radical revaluing of her society

can leave even her critics stumbling behind her and it also shows that such revaluing characterizes the stories every bit as much as it does the novels.

8

The Achievement of Jean Rhys

Phoebe, altering her expectations and deciding to be bad, reifies the values of her society even as she contemplates rebelling against them. For to fall is, of course, to delineate most graphically the safe ground on which one no longer stands; it is to serve as an object lesson to other women of what they must not be; it is to serve, too, as the sacrificial victim whose vice makes possible–given the conventional double standard–the virtue of those other proper women. Phoebe thus anticipates not just the demimonde adult life of the author but also a crucial and seemingly contradictory quality in all of Jean Rhys's adult protagonists. From Anna who loves Walter and would accept him on practically any terms to Antoinette who loves Rochester in much the same abject manner, Rhys again and again portrays women who knowingly participate in their own victimization. They experience the gross injustices that their society so easily inflicts on women, they often explicitly and eloquently lament these injustices, and yet they also persistently embrace them. It is difficult to decide just what we should make of such accommodating sufferers.

The problem is compounded when we note how effectively Rhys departs from the standard formulae for portraying females both in accord with and in opposition to their society. The oldest and most established of such formulae is the contrast of the virtuous girl versus the unvirtuous one, with virtue or its loss being essentially synonymous with virginity or its loss. A retained maidenhead ostensibly qualifies one for honorable wedlock and happiness ever after, while its premature misplacement supposedly assures disgrace, disease, and a disgusting death. As already indicated, Rhys recognizes the conventional disposition of these different ladies as a pernicious myth that validates patriarchal power and reduces women to, at best, a kind of commodity, and, at worst, to human garbage. Yet, as we have also observed, this same myth ironically informs Rhys's fiction. Anna could not have been abandoned by Walter Jeffries, by Carl Redman, by the nameless men who came after those two had she not also gone to bed with them all; Mr. Mackenzie would not get off so easily had his promises to Julia been made before a clergyman; even Antoinette, any Victorian novelist or contemporary sexologist might maintain, was too forward for her own good and thus put off the man. In short, Rhys's unhappy protagonists evince standard reasons for standard suffering, yet the author still somehow denies the standard interpretation of that state of affairs.

The values affirmed by the different fortunes of the mistress of the manor and the mistress of the night have been often condemned by other writers, so here too some conventions for portraying female characters (woman now as rebel) have arisen. Begin with an especially capable woman who properly represses most of her abilities; dramatize the unfair burdens under which she labors all the harder in that she labors duplicitously, attempting to succeed while avoiding the appearance of success; show her finally refusing the demeaning role she is supposed to play. The great prototype for this character and resolution is seen in Ibsen's "A Doll's House" when Nora Helmer slams the door on her husband Torvald's home and strides off into the larger world. And Rhys also both employs this formula and subverts it. Her characters stride bravely off into the larger world too, but they stride to a different end than Nora's. In effect, the action in Rhys's novels continues considerably beyond the final curtain of Ibsen's play to show that the social edifice does not come tumbling down with one slammed door. Rhys's early protagonists in particular discover a whole world filled with Torvald houses, a world in which the one house they were intent on escaping begins to appear in retrospect almost as paradise lost. It is as if Nora comes back several years later to hang around her former home, hoping to catch a glimpse of the children but knowing that her leaving has precluded her from ever claiming again the place she once had. The woman in conventional revolt has become the conventionally fallen woman. One formula undermines and contradicts the other.

Judith Thurman rightly observes that "one of the most terrifying aspects of Jean Rhys's heroine is the debasement of her solitude—a solitude which was, at its outset, audacious and brave, but which she has acknowledged as a defeat, even as a punishment."[1] For Thurman, this "defeat" produces a "squalid complicity" between the woman and the men who use her. She barters for "their company, their protection, their money," and pays with "the pleasure she can give them as a victim." Thurman also suggests that this desperate solution to desperate loneliness characterizes "modern woman . . . on her own, the woman who has renounced 'respectability'—the protection of a father or husband—and who is, in society's eyes, without a place, illegitimate and therefore fair game for the presumptions of men."[2]

This convincing assessment of the defeated woman's plight is not, however, carried far enough. For example, the "squalid complicity" between victim and victimizer was there all along and was, indeed, what prompted the protagonist's brave foray on her own. Furthermore, and in another sense, the woman always was on her own.

Renouncing "respectability" was not renouncing her place in society, it was renouncing society's attempt to place her; and with that place defined by those other than herself, by those in power, she has ever been fair game for the presumptions of men. In brief, and just as it should do, the protagonist's fall shows her–and us–exactly where she was standing when the fall took place. Rhys thus erases the very formulaic oppositions out of which she structures the text, and the virtuous rewarded woman, the punished vicious woman, the woman in brave revolt, and the abjectly defeated woman are all finally the same woman. In that conflation of characters we see another odd conjunction. For Rhys, the conventional justifications for the working of society constitute its most damning indictments.

Differently put, I am arguing that Rhys calculatingly works out a double perspective whereby two visions that should ostensibly be quite different turn out to be very much the same. We can assess society from the perspective of the author's alienated female protagonists, or we can assess those protagonists from the perspective of generally accepted social values. Presumably most of Rhys's readers and critics are more committed to social norms than to radical alienation and so are more likely to employ the second perspective than the first.[3] Yet that second perspective readily brings in the first, as two brief examples can amply attest.

To consider first one of Rhys's first critics, Elgin Mellown maintains that the very proper future which Phoebe renounces in "Goodbye Marcus, Goodbye Rose" constitutes the one sure cure for all that ails Rhys's unhappy heroines. This critic argues that the Rhys "woman never finds a man who will faithfully continue to fulfill her needs," and that lacking the proper love (marital and monogamous) of a good man, she also lacks the proper product of that love: "These tortured women cannot reach maturity by giving birth to a child which, depending on them, will force them into adulthood; and having no husbands to provide for them and no way of earning a living other than by selling their bodies . . . they must abort any life that may spring in their wombs."[4] No husband in her bed, no baby in her cradle, no wonder–the implicit argument runs–the Rhys woman has lost her moorings. For Rhys, however, and for Phoebe, this prescribed cure is the essence of the disease. A woman's "saving" moorings can also tie her down for life.

Mellown's analysis of the outcast status of Rhys's "archetypal woman" does, indeed, merely speak the traditional double standard in which that analysis is based. Thus, even though he praises Rhys for being "one of the first women writers to express an unabashed, direct acceptance of woman's desire for sexual love," Mellown also intimates that in Rhys's fiction such desire regularly gets out of hand: "Instinctively knowing that her man will desert her, the woman increasingly debases herself in a desperate attempt to hold on to him, the inevitable result being that her abandoned position increases his revulsion. The Rhys woman may be a mistress in name, but in fact she is always a victim of love because she is at the mercy of her uncontrollable desires."[5] Somehow the passage that begins by noting the woman's knowledge that her man will inevitably leave her ends by attributing her eventual desertion to her own wayward impulses, not to his. And equally dubious is Mellown's assumption that the only viable road to female maturity is necessarily paved with dirty diapers. This critic, who does regard Rhys as a major writer, cannot grant her characters any grounds for their rebellions against their society. Those characters cannot claim any such ground either, and it is precisely their failure which helps us to recognize another version of their denied humanity as set forth by Mellown.

Or we might notice a more recent critic's contention

that "the Rhys heroine is a natural victim, not a victim of sexual politics or class oppression."[6] Yet sexual politics and class oppression both naturally produce their natural victims. What is "natural" cannot be helped, and it is always a comforting thought that the lower orders are situated exactly where they should be, where they deserve to be, so that not even sympathy need be expended on their behalf. Indeed, "towards the heroine of [Rhys's] novels," Linda Bamber actually argues, "we may surely be permitted to feel some irritation and disapproval."[7] As Marya observes in *Quartet*, the strong require victims in order to "exercise their will and become more strong." With such passages, Rhys underlines and emphasizes, in Thurman's phrasing, "the brutality inherent in all privilege."[8] Bamber, postulating natural victims, underlines that underlining even as she also unintentionally emphasizes how unnatural those victims are. To quote a far more perceptive assessment of victimization in Rhys's fiction: "To be female is to inhabit, without hope of escape, the lowest class of all in a sexist structure."[9]

"Why write about slack, self-indulgent women who practice no skill and throw away money on clothes and drink?" Peter Wolfe asks.[10] He has a good answer to the question that other critics have asked less rhetorically: "The heroines in Jane Austen, Henry James, and Elizabeth Bowen all belong in the liberal-humanist tradition. Jean Rhys's culture-starved women are harder to write about. Yet there are fifty Julia Martins walking our sidewalks for every Elizabeth Bennett or Isabel Archer. We see them every day and barely notice them. By presenting them honestly and by withholding judgment Jean Rhys has sharpened our understanding of daily reality."[11] Rhys has done that and much besides, for we do not read her just to encounter a hitherto neglected type, to recognize a social or emotional bag lady should we meet with one. To see more is to see differently. The madwoman in the attic has, of course, been put there not to be seen. Yet to examine this outcast's case is to call into question all the conventions that define such characters as marginal. Indeed, for Rhys, these "marginal" women are situated exactly at the heart of the matter and shadow forth the essence of the world they inhabit. It is therefore most appropriate that Sandra M. Gilbert and Susan Gubar gave their seminal work the title of *The Madwoman in the Attic*, for Jean Rhys, although she was reluctant to describe herself as a feminist, anticipates, encourages, and validates much contemporary feminist criticism.

We read Rhys, V. S. Naipaul has suggested, to see the whole world reflected in her "woman's half-world," the "*demi-monde*" that takes its "exact meaning" from "exile and dependence."[12] As Naipaul concludes: "Out of her fidelity to her experience and her purity as a novelist, Jean Rhys thirty to forty years ago identified many of the themes that engage us today: isolation, an absence of society or community, the sense of things falling apart, dependence, loss. Her achievement is very grand."[13] We read her, too, because what she writes she writes superlatively well, with a prose "reticent, unemphatic, precise, and yet supple, alive with feeling, as though the whole world she so cooly describes were shimmering with foreboding, with a lifetime's knowledge of unease and pain."[14] We read her because of the personal triumph whereby that life of pain was transmuted and transcended. As much as any modern author, Rhys turned the transitory disasters of a disordered and mismanaged life into works of enduring art. And we read her, I would finally suggest, because of the paradoxical hope prompted by her hopeless fiction. It will be remembered that Hester Prynne at the end of *The Scarlet Letter* was presented, over a hundred years ago, as a prophet of a better future. "A new truth would be revealed," Hester assured her fellow unhappy sufferers (Puritans in the text, Victorians of Hawthorne's time, and in both cases, no doubt, mostly women). This truth would "establish the whole relation between man and woman on a surer ground of mutual happiness." Rhys was a different prophet, a prophet of a present unhappiness as securely founded as any past ones on "the whole relation between man and woman." Her present speaks more persuasively than Hester's promise and thus might still nudge us in that direction after all.

Notes

1. FROM DOMINICA TO OBSCURITY AND FAME

1.   David Plante, *Difficult Women: A Memoir of Three* (New York: Atheneum, 1983), 19.
2.   From Diana Athill's "Foreword" to Jean Rhys, *Smile Please: An Unfinished Autobiography* (New York: Harper and Row, 1979), 6.
3.   The dividing line between fiction and fact is, of course, always problematic in autobiographies. As Elizabeth W. Bruss observes, in *Autobiographical Acts: The Changing Situation of a Literary Genre* (Baltimore: The Johns Hopkins University Press, 1976), 128, the necessary fiction at the roots of fact and the interests behind disinterested empiricism places autobiography in a difficult position. "What is it," she goes on to ask, "that autobiography actually captures? How much does it record and how much does it create?"
4.   The interrelationship between Rhys's novel and her autobiography is still more complicated, it should be noted, in that *Voyage in the Dark* was based not just on memories but also on a journal account of the affair that Rhys wrote shortly after the event and then kept with her until, some twenty years later, it could be used for writing the novel.
5.   Todd K. Bender, in "Jean Rhys," *Contemporary Literature*, 22 (1981), 249–52, stresses the need for a comprehensive biography and specifies the hard questions that such a work should answer.
6.   Arnold E. Davidson, *Mordecai Richler* (New York: Frederick Ungar, 1983), 3.

7. Plante, for example, reports Rhys's insistence that "nothing else is important" but the "writing" (22).

8. Ford Madox Ford, "Preface" to *The Left Bank and Other Stories* by Jean Rhys (London: Jonathan Cape, 1927), 24.

9. Louis James, *Jean Rhys* (London: Longman, 1978), 33.

10. James, 34.

11. Ford had earlier edited the *English Review* in London and had already established himself as an important discoverer of new talent.

12. For a full account of Ford Madox Ford's disordered life, see Arthur Mizener, *The Saddest Story: A Biography of Ford Madox Ford* (New York: World Publishing, 1971).

13. As Bender (249–50) points out, the question of just how and how much Ford influenced Rhys's writing is one of the crucial problems that a comprehensive biography should answer.

14. But Ford apparently took more credit than he was entitled to, for Rhys's 1928 translation of Francis Carco's *Perversity* was published under Ford's name.

15. A. Alvarez, "The Best Living English Novelist," *New York Times Book Review*, 17 March 1974, 7–8.

16. The affair with Ford, for example, is not even mentioned in *Smile Please*.

2. *Wide Sargasso Sea:*
REMODELING THE HOUSE OF FICTION

11. Todd K. Bender, "*Jean Rhys*," *Contemporary Literature*, 22 (1981), 250.

12. Walter Allen, "Bertha the Doomed," A Review of *Wide Sargasso Sea*, *New York Times Book Review*, 18 June 1967, 5.

13. For excellent recent discussions of *Jane Eyre*, see Helene Moglen, *Charlotte Brontë: The Self Conceived* (New York: Norton, 1976), 105–45; and Sandra M. Gilbert and Susan Gubar, *The Madwoman in the Attic: The Woman Writer and the Nineteenth-Century Literary Imagination* (New Haven: Yale University Press, 1979), 336–71.

14. "She seemed such a poor ghost, I thought I'd like to write

her life," Rhys observed in an interview, as quoted by
Michael Thorpe, "'The Other Side': *Wide Sargasso Sea*
and *Jane Eyre*," *ARIEL*, 8, no. 3 (1977), 99.

5. Rosalind Miles, *The Fiction of Sex: Themes and Functions
    of Sex Differences in the Modern Novel* (New York:
    Barnes and Noble, 1974), 55.

6. Gilbert and Gubar, 360.

7. Ronnie Scharfman, "Mirroring and Mothering in Simone
    Schwarz-Bart's *Pluie et vent sur Télumée Miracle* and Jean
    Rhys' *Wide Sargasso Sea*," *Yale French Studies*, 62 (1981),
    100.

8. Helen Nebeker, *Jean Rhys: Woman in Passage* (Montreal:
    Eden Press, 1981), 159.

9. See Phyllis Chesler, *Woman and Madness* (New York:
    Doubleday, 1972).

10. Walter Allen (5), for example, describes the Rhys pro-
    tagonist as a young woman "who is hopelessly and
    helplessly at sea in her relations with men, a passive victim,
    doomed to destruction"; and some fifteen years later
    Linda Bamber, in "Jean Rhys," *Partisan Review*, 49, no. 1
    (1982), 94, strikes an even more critically condescending
    note: "The Rhys heroine knows that she is largely respon-
    sible for her own unhappiness. Whenever something good
    comes her way—money, a man, the possibility of a good
    time—she instantly loses it through laziness, obsessive-
    ness, or a kind of petty anger arising from her sense that it
    isn't enough."

11. Clara Thomas, "Mr. Rochester's First Marriage: *Wide
    Sargasso Sea* by Jean Rhys," *World Literature Written in
    English*, 17 (1978), 348.

12. The large dowry, it should be noted, does not demonstrate
    that Antoinette has somehow been wealthy all along. The
    money was left by her stepfather, who was, perhaps,
    prompted by belated guilt for the way he had treated
    Antoinette's mother. And after Mr. Mason's death the
    thirty thousand pounds is administered by Richard
    Mason, a son by another marriage and Antoinette's step-
    brother.

13. Todd K. Bender, "Jean Rhys and the Genius of Impre-

ssionism," *Studies in the Literary Imagination*, 11. no. 2 (1978), 45.

14. Peter Wolfe, in *Jean Rhys* (Boston: Twayne, 1980), 142, notes Rochester's "pawn complex."

15. Not only did Antoinette have no voice in arranging the terms of the marriage, her interests were not looked after either. Richard Mason, the stepbrother, refuses to heed warnings that the girl's dowry should be at least in part secured for her through a legal settlement, as was the stepfather's "intention." Richard insists that Rochester is "an honourable gentleman," and "I would trust him with my life." But as Antoinette's capable Aunt Cora points out, Richard is "trusting him with [Antoinette's] life, not [his own].

16. Nebeker, 125.

17. The reader can also note other evidence of hypocrisy, such as his obvious disapproval of any signs of affection between Antoinette and her old nurse, Christophine–"*I* wouldn't hug and kiss them . . . I couldn't"–expressed shortly before he does rather more than just hug and kiss Amélie.

18. This juxtaposing is further complicated by the fact that Rochester would prefer his wife to be both mad and exclusively his–to "give herself as no sane woman would" but only to him–and that state ("mad but *mine, mine*") is totally self-contradictory according to his own definitions of sanity, sex, and matrimony.

19. Thorpe, 109.

20. Thomas, 355.

21. The same basic point is made by Elizabeth Abel in "Women and Schizophrenia: The Fiction of Jean Rhys," *Contemporary Literature*, 20 (1979), 173: "By identifying Rochester with attempted rationality and objectivity and Antoinette with intuition and subjectivity, Rhys dramatizes the interaction of two fundamentally different ways of ordering experience, and by subtly reinforcing Antoinette's perceptions, she forces us to re-examine our response to madness."

22. Scharfman, 104.

23.   Louis James, *Jean Rhys* (London: Longman, 1978), 62.

24.   Scharfman, 105.

25.   Mary Lou Emery, "The Politics of Form: Jean Rhys's Social Vision in *Voyage in the Dark* and *Wide Sargasso Sea*," *Twentieth Century Literature*, 28 (1982), 428.

26.   Emery, 428–29.

27.   As Abel notes, there is a "growing emphasis on women's relationships" in Rhys's fiction (176).

28.   T. S. Eliot, *Selected Prose of T. S. Eliot*, ed. Frank Kermode (New York: Harcourt Brace Jovanovich, 1975), 38–39.

29.   Bender, "Jean Rhys," 250.

30.   Gilbert and Gubar point out that the "physical isolation" of Rochester and Jane at the end of *Jane Eyre* helps them "to circumvent the strictures of a hierarchal society" and forge a union of equals (369). The comparable isolation of the earlier pair of lovers hardly worked in the same way.

31.   For a much more extended discussion of such bias (but a discussion limited to American texts), see Judith Fetterley, *The Resisting Reader: A Feminist Approach to American Fiction* (Bloomington: Indiana University Press, 1978).

32.   Emery, 429.

3. *Voyage in the Dark:*
The Early Tragedies of the Rhys Protagonist

1.   For example, Peter Wolfe, in *Jean Rhys* (Boston: Twayne, 1980), 120, finds *Voyage in the Dark* to be "Rhys's most beautiful, dangerous, and, in view of its grimness, distressingly clear novel"; Rhys incidentally, according to Thomas Staley in *Jean Rhys* (Austin: University of Texas Press, 1979), 8, also regarded *Voyage in the Dark* as "the favorite of her novels."

2.   The first brief quotation is from Elgin W. Mellown, "Character and Themes in the Novels of Jean Rhys," *Contemporary Literature*, 13 (1972), 460; the second is from Harriet Blodgett, "Tigers Are Better Looking to Jean Rhys," *Arizona Quarterly*, 32 (1976), 28–29.

3. Louis James, *Jean Rhys* (London: Longman, 1978), 40.

4. Helen Nebeker, it might be noted, argues, in *Jean Rhys: Woman in Passage* (Montreal: Eden Press, 1981), 74–78, that some kind of sexual fall brought Anna from the West Indies to England, and hence the whole novel represents a failed attempt at a new beginning. This interpretation is suggestive but is not clearly supported by the text.

5. For a fuller discussion of the moral and social significance of the seduction novel see G. B. Needham and R. P. Utter, *Pamela's Daughters* (Berkeley: University of California Press, 1936); or Mary Kelley, "The Sentimentalists: Promise and Betrayal in the Home," *Signs*, 4 (1979), 434–46.

6. A. Alvarez, "The Best Living English Novelist," *New York Times Book Review*, 17 March 1974, 7.

7. Nebeker, 54–55.

8. Nebeker, 55.

9. As Staley (63) observes, Walter "plays the role of seducer with consummate skill." The essence of that skill, of course, is not to seem to be playing the role.

10. Wolfe, 106.

11. She has previously always been sent back to her room alone in the early morning after spending part of the night with Walter.

12. Nebeker, 51.

13. Francis Hope, "Women Beware Everyone," *Observer Review*, 11 June 1967, 24; quoted by Wolfe, 111.

14. He also, it should be added, offers this last help only on the condition that she returns all his letters.

15. Todd Bender, "Jean Rhys and the Genius of Impressionism," *Studies in the Literary Imagination*, 11, no. 2 (1978), 52.

16. Bender, 52. But it should be noted that Walter was already "set on deserting" Anna and that Germaine didn't laugh. Her response was, "Bravo kid."

4. *Quartet*: THE FICTION OF A MENAGE A TROIS

1. Helen Nebeker, in *Jean Rhys: Woman in Passage*

(Montreal: Eden Press, 1981), 1, describes this general condemnation but does not agree with it. "*Quartet,*" she goes on to observe in the same passage, gives us "our first glimpse of Rhys's complexity and latent genius."

2. Elgin W. Mellown, "Character and Themes in the Novels of Jean Rhys," *Contemporary Literature*, 13 (1972), 463; and Harriet Blodgett, "Tigers are Better Looking to Jean Rhys," *Arizona Quarterly*, 32 (1976), 232.

3. Diana Athill reports this statement in a letter to Helen Nebeker and quoted in Nebeker (44).

4. Peter Wolfe, *Jean Rhys* (Boston: Twayne, 1980), 82.

5. Thomas Staley, *Jean Rhys* (Austin: University of Texas Press, 1979), 35.

6. Frank Baldanza, "Jean Rhys on Insult and Injury," *Studies in the Literary Imagination*, 11, no. 2 (1978), 59.

7. Nebeker, 3.

8. Mellown, 460.

9. Mellown, 461.

10. Diana Athill, in her "Foreword" to *Smile Please* (New York: Harper and Row, 1979), 9, reports that Rhys, who translated the novel and helped to arrange for its English publication out of a sense of what was "only fair," admitted to cutting "a few—a very few—sentences about herself which struck her as 'too unfair.'"

11. Stella Bowen, *Drawn from Life: Reminiscences* (London: Collins, 1941), 166–67. But Bowen also records "the other side of the balance," the other woman's "bad health, destitution, shattered nerves . . . and a complete absence of any desire for independence."

12. Paul Delany, "Jean Rhys and Ford Madox Ford: What 'Really' Happened," *Mosaic*, 16, no. 4 (1983), 16. Delany also observes that Ford's *When the Wicked Man* (1931) is a "retrospective" fictionalizing of the affair but one that simply "caricatures" Rhys to produce "one of Ford's weakest novels" (17).

13. Judith Kegan Gardiner, "Rhys Recalls Ford: *Quartet* and *The Good Soldier*," *Tulsa Studies in Women's Literature*, 1 (1982), 67.

14. Ford Madox Ford, "Preface" to *The Left Bank and Other*

Stories by Jean Rhys (London: Jonathan Cape, 1927), 24.

15. Gardiner, 67 and 80. *The Good Soldier*, it should be remembered, is subtitled *A Tale of Passion*, and Ford originally intended to title the work "The Saddest Story."

16. Staley, 39.

17. Staley, 40.

18. As Wolfe observes, Heidler is "a socially acceptable version of . . . Stephan" (75).

19. Wolfe, 76.

20. Wolfe, 74.

21. Considering these actions, it is hard to agree with Nebeker's claim that, "at the novel's conclusion, it is Stephan with whom we sympathize" (12).

22. Mellown, for example, maintains that "the novel ends in a flurry of melodrama" (461); Blodgett similarly criticizes its "melodramatic finale" (233).

5. THE ART AND ECONOMICS OF DESTITUTION IN *Leaving Mr. Mackenzie*

1. Thomas Staley, in *Jean Rhys* (Austin: University of Texas Press, 1979), 68, describes *After Leaving Mr. Mackenzie* as a "portrayal of a woman" at "the nadir of her existence."

2. Thus Frank Baldanza, in "Jean Rhys on Insult and Injury," *Studies in the Literary Imagination*, 11, no. 2 (1978), 60, notes Julia's "admirably integral grittiness" and her "assertion of her own autonomy in the face of impossibly bleak prospects."

3. Staley, 69.

4. Peter Wolfe, *Jean Rhys* (Boston: Twayne, 1980), 88.

5. The point that I am making here is made in slightly different form by Wolfe who emphasizes how much Julia's life is shown as "wheeling in circles" (99). More recently and more specifically, Henrik Mossin, in "The Existentialist Dimension in the Novels of Jean Rhys," *Kunapipi*, 3, no. 1 (1981), 145, has argued that this picture "indicates the central image of the novel, that of the cycle, representing the circular movement of existence, in which progressive

development is only carving out the essence of past experiences."

6. As Helen Nebeker points out in *Jean Rhys: Woman in Passage* (Montreal: Eden Press, 1981), 31, "Julia totally ignores the fact that for years her sister has borne the burden of their mother and poverty while she, at least, has had the opportunity to search for something better."

7. Wolfe, 95.

8. As Staley observes, Julia's "constant search for money" signifies "on a deeper level . . . her quest for some human engagement" (69).

9. P. A. Packer, "The Four Early Novels of Jean Rhys," *Durham University Journal*, 71 (1979), 257.

10. That Julia ended the affair with Horsefield before it ran its full course is still another positive note.

11. Nebeker, 34–36.

12. I quote from Rebecca West's brief evaluation of the novel, which is itself quoted by Wolfe (101).

6. AFFIRMATION FROM DESPAIR IN
Good Morning, Midnight

1. Thomas F. Staley, *Jean Rhys: A Critical Study* (Austin: University of Texas Press, 1979), 97.

2. Frank Baldanza, "Jean Rhys on Insult and Injury," *Studies in the Literary Imagination*, 11, no. 2 (1978), 65.

3. Peter Wolfe, *Jean Rhys* (Boston: Twayne, 1980), 135.

4. Wolfe, 134.

5. Elgin W. Mellown, "Character and Themes in the Novels of Jean Rhys," *Contemporary Literature*, 13 (1972), 467.

6. Mellown, 467.

7. Baldanza, 64.

8. Mellown, 464.

9. Stella Bowen, *Drawn From Life: Reminiscences* (London: Collins, 1941), 166.

10. Staley, 84.

11. Elizabeth Abel, "Women and Schizophrenia: The Fiction of Jean Rhys," *Contemporary Literature*, 20 (1979), 156. I

would also argue that Abel's diagnosis of Sasha as a schizophrenic often seems strained. To consider just one example, the painting of, ostensibly, a "doubleheaded, double-faced, banjo player" (Abel, 163) is described in the novel as simply a portrait of "an old Jew with a red nose, playing the banjo." Far from showing the protagonist's propensities towards *The Divided Self* (the R. D. Laing formulation of schizophrenia with which Abel underpins her argument), Sasha's choice of this painting simply demonstrates her affinity for the outcast and downtrodden, especially when they can still make music. Basically, the objective world *is*, for Sasha, "obdurate and antagonistic"; it is not, as Abel implies, rendered so by "her fragile consciousness" (164).

12. Mellown, 462.

13. Mellown, 462; and Harriet Blodgett, "Tigers are Better Looking to Jean Rhys," *Arizona Quarterly*, 32 (1976), 240.

14. Mellown, 467. The gigolo, it will be recalled, identifies himself as "a French-Canadian."

15. Mellown, 462.

16. An excellent example of this process is Sasha's memory of the man who tried to seduce her with the sympathy-evoking tale of how his mistress had crassly implored him to buy her a new pair of shoes and who is then completely put off and flees in disgust when he elicits from Sasha the observation that she has not eaten in a week.

17. Staley, 93.

18. Louis James, *Jean Rhys* (London: Longman, 1978), 28.

19. That past envisaging is especially summed up by the action immediately preceding the beginning of the novel, Sasha's attempt to drink herself to death.

20. Staley, 93.

21. Staley, 92.

22. Wolfe, 133.

23. Staley, 96.

24. Some critics have tended to glide, like René, over the obvious implications of his words and actions during this scene. Thus Baldanza, for example, observes that "he

threatens violence because, though an obvious gigolo, his male pride is piqued" (65)–as if pique should justify a sexual assault.

25. She had earlier teased him about his unlikely prospects for making a fortune by selling himself to the frustrated wives of generally asexual–or so he dreams–Englishmen.

26. Abel, 167.

27. Wolfe, 135.

7. FROM The Left Bank TO Sleep It Off, Lady OTHER VERSIONS OF DISORDERED LIFE

1. This point is somewhat differently made by Ford Madox Ford in his preface when he notes that he "tried . . . very hard to induce the author of *The Left Bank* to introduce some sort of topography of that region . . . into her sketches," but "once her attention was called to the matter, she eliminated even such two or three words of descriptive matter as had crept into her work. Her business was with passion, hardship, emotions: the locality in which these things are endured is immaterial."

2. The name of the hotel, given in the last words of the text, is, "Nach London," which suggests that the protagonist's life will continue to be, in the future and in other European cities, much as it was in the past and in Vienna, Budapest, and Prague.

3. Thomas F. Staley, *Jean Rhys: A Critical Study* (Austin: University of Texas Press, 1979), 30.

4. Peter Wolfe, *Jean Rhys* (Boston: Twayne, 1980), 41.

5. Staley, 31.

6. One man may drive out another, but so too can one woman replace another woman or one suffering replace another suffering. Indeed, at the conclusion of the story, Fifi's loss of love is ended by her loss of life.

7. Judith Thurman, "The Mistress and the Mask: Jean Rhys's Fiction," *Ms.,* January 1976, 81.

8. Wolfe, 60.

9. Wolfe, 53.

10. Staley, 126.

11. And by the same logic Wolfe's postulation that "her lover-comforter has died to let her live" (54) is equally dubious.

12. A. C. Morrell, "The World of Jean Rhys's Short Stories," *World Literature Written in English*, 18 (1979), 242.

13. Wolfe, 47.

14. Morrell, 243.

15. Rosalind Miles, *The Fiction of Sex: Themes and Functions of Sex Difference in the Modern Novel* (New York: Barnes and Noble, 1974), 99.

16. Morrell, 238.

17. Wolfe, 62, 63, and 66.

18. Wolfe, 163.

19. Staley, 129.

20. Staley, 129.

21. Staley, 129.

8. THE ACHIEVEMENT OF JEAN RHYS

1. Judith Thurman, "The Mistress and the Mask: Jean Rhys's Fiction," *Ms.*, January 1976, 51.

2. Thurman, 51.

3. Judith Kegan Gardiner, in "Good Morning, Midnight; Good Night, Modernism," *Boundary 2*, 11 (1982/83), 233, has recently described Jean Rhys as "one of the greatest novelists of alienation" and has also rightly observed that "the alienation of her characters has alienated some of her critics who wish to exclude themselves from the experiences about which she writes."

4. Elgin W. Mellown, "Character and Themes in the Novels of Jean Rhys," *Contemporary Literature*, 13 (1972), 464.

5. Mellown, 464.

6. Linda Bamber, "Jean Rhys," *Partisan Review*, 49, no. 1 (1982), 94.

7. Bamber, 100.

8. Thurman, 50.

9. Rosalind Miles, *The Fiction of Sex: Themes and Functions of Sex Difference in the Modern Novel* (New York: Barnes and Noble, 1974), 99.

10. Peter Wolfe, *Jean Rhys* (Boston: Twayne, 1980), 29.

11. Wolfe, 31.
12. V. S. Naipaul, "Without a Dog's Chance," *New York Review of Books*, 18 May 1972, 30.
13. Naipaul, 31.
14. A. Alvarez, "The Best Living English Novelist," *New York Times Book Review*, 17 March 1974, 7; and Irene Thompson, in "The Left Bank Apéritifs of Jean Rhys and Ernest Hemingway," *The Georgia Review*, 35 (1981), 96–97, quotes in more detail the high praise that has been bestowed on Rhys as a master prose stylist.

Bibliography

BOOKS BY JEAN RHYS

The Left Bank and Other Stories. London: Jonathan Cape, 1927.

Postures. London: Chatto and Windus, 1928; published in America as *Quartet*: New York: Simon and Schuster, 1929 (and now republished in both England and America as *Quartet*).

After Leaving Mr. Mackenzie. London: Jonathan Cape, 1931.

Voyage in the Dark. London: Constable, 1934.

Good Morning, Midnight. London: Constable, 1939.

Wide Sargasso Sea. London: André Deutsch, 1966.

Tigers Are Better-Looking. London: André Deutsch, 1968.

My Day. New York: Frank Hallman, 1975.

Sleep It Off, Lady. London: André Deutsch, 1976.

Smile Please: An Unfinished Biography. New York: Harper and Row, 1979.

SELECTED CRITICISMS

Abel, Elizabeth. "Women and Schizophrenia: The Fiction of Jean Rhys." *Contemporary Literature* 20 (1979), 155–77.

Alvarez, Alfred. "The Best Living English Novelist." *New York Times Book Review*, 17 March 1974, 6–8.

Baldanza, Frank. "Jean Rhys on Insult and Injury." *Studies in the Literary Imagination* 11, no. 2 (1978), 55–65.

Bamber, Linda. "Jean Rhys." *Partisan Review* 49, no. 1 (1982), 92–100.

Bender, Todd K. "Jean Rhys and the Genius of Impressionism." *Studies in the Literary Imagination* 11, no. 2 (1978), 43–53.

———. "Jean Rhys." *Contemporary Literature* 22 (1981), 248–52.

Blodgett, Harriet. "Tigers Are Better Looking to Jean Rhys." *Arizona Quarterly* 32 (1976), 227–44.

Dash, Cheryl M. L. "Jean Rhys." In *West Indian Literature*, edited by Bruce King, pp. 196–239. London: Macmillan, 1979.

Davidson, Arnold E. "The Dark is Light Enough: Affirmation from Despair in Jean Rhys's *Good Morning, Midnight*." *Contemporary Literature* 24 (1983), 349–64.

———. "The Art and Economics of Destitution in Jean Rhys's *After Leaving Mr. Mackenzie*." *Studies in the Novel*, 16 (1984), 215–27.

Delany, Paul. "Jean Rhys and Ford Madox Ford: What 'Really' Happened." *Mosaic* 16, no. 4 (1983), 15–24.

Emery, Mary Lou. "The Politics of Form: Jean Rhys's Social Vision in *Voyage in the Dark* and *Wide Sargasso Sea*." *Twentieth Century Literature* 28 (1982), 418–30.

Gardiner, Judith Kegan. "Rhys Recalls Ford: *Quartet* and *The Good Soldier*." *Tulsa Studies in Women's Literature* 1 (1982), 67–81.

———. "Good Morning, Midnight; Good Night, Modernism," *Boundary 2*, 11 (1982/83), 233–51.

Harris, Wilson. "Carnival of Psyche: Jean Rhys's *Wide Sargasso Sea*." *Kunapipi* 2, no. 2 (1980), 142–50.

James, Louis. "Sun Fire–Painted Fire: Jean Rhys as a Caribbean Novelist." *ARIEL* 8, no. 3 (1977), 111–27.

———. *Jean Rhys*. London: Longman, 1978.

Look Lai, Wally. "The Road to Thornfield Hall: An Analysis of Jean Rhys's *Wide Sargasso Sea*." In *New Beacon Reviews*, edited by John La Rose, 38–52. London: New Beacon Books Ltd., 1968.

Luengo, Anthony E. "*Wide Sargasso Sea* and the Gothic Mode." *World Literature Written in English* 15 (1976), 229–45.

Mellown, Elgin W. "Character and Themes in The Novels of Jean Rhys." *Contemporary Literature* 13 (1972), 458–75.

———. "A Bibliography of the Writings of Jean Rhys with a Selected List of Reviews and Other Critical Writings." *World Literature Written in English* 16 (1977), 179–202.

Miles, Rosalind. *The Fiction of Sex: Themes and Functions of Sex Difference in the Modern Novel*, pp. 96–106. New York: Barnes and Noble, 1974.

Morrell, A. C. "The World of Jean Rhys's Short Stories." *World Literature Written in English* 18 (1979), 235–44.

Mossin, Henrik. "The Existential Dimension in the Novels of Jean Rhys." *Kunapipi* 3, no. 1 (1981), 143–50.

Naipaul, V. S. "Without a Dog's Chance." *New York Review of Books*, 18 May 1972, 29–31.

Nebeker, Helen E. "Jean Rhys's *Quartet*: The Genesis of Myth." *International Journal of Women's Studies* 2 (1979), 257–67.

———. *Jean Rhys: Woman in Passage*. Montreal: Eden Press, 1981.

Packer, P. A. "The Four Early Novels of Jean Rhys." *Durham University Journal* 71 (1979), 252–65.

Plante, David. *Difficult Women: A Memoir of Three*, pp. 9–61.New York: Atheneum, 1983.

Pool, Gail. "Jean Rhys: Life's Unfinished Form." *Chicago Review* 32, no. 4 (1981), 68–74.

Porter, Dennis. "Of Heroines and Victims: Jean Rhys and *Jane Eyre*." *Massachusetts Review* 17 (1976), 540–52.

Scharfman, Ronnie. Mirroring and Mothering in Simone Schwarz-Bart's *Pluie et vent sur Télumée Miracle* and Jean Rhys's *Wide Sargasso Sea*." *Yale French Studies* 62 (1981), 88–106.

Staley, Thomas F. "The Emergence of a Form: Style and Consciousness in Jean Rhys's *Quartet*." *Twentieth Century Literature* 24 (1978), 202–24.

———. *Jean Rhys: A Critical Study*. Austin: University of Texas Press, 1979.

Thomas, Clara. "Mr. Rochester's First Marriage: *Wide Sargasso Sea* by Jean Rhys." *World Literature Written in English* 17 (1978), 342–57.

Thompson, Irene. "The Left Bank Apéritifs of Jean Rhys and Ernest Hemingway." *Georgia Review* 35 (1981), 94–106.

Thorpe, Michael. "'The Other Side': *Wide Sargasso Sea* and *Jane Eyre*." *ARIEL* 8, no. 3 (1977), 99–110.

Thurman, Judith. "The Mistress and the Mask: Jean Rhys's Fiction." *Ms.*, January 1976, 50–53, 81.

Tiffin, Helen. "Mirror and Mask: Colonial Motifs in the Novels of Jean Rhys." *World Literature Written in English* 17 (1978), 328–41.

Vreeland, Elizabeth. "Jean Rhys: The Art of Fiction [Interview] LXIV." *Paris Review* 21, no. 76 (1979), 218–37.

Wolfe, Peter. *Jean Rhys*. Boston: Twayne, 1980.

Wyndham, Francis. "Introduction to Jean Rhys." *The London Magazine*, 7 January 1960, 15–18; and reprinted as the introduction to *Wide Sargasso Sea*.

Index